The Stay-at-Home Dad Handbook

Peter Baylies

with Jessica Toonkel

CHICAGO REVIEW PRESS

Library of Congress Cataloging-in-Publication Data
Baylies, Peter.
The stay-at-home dad handbook / Peter Baylies with Jessica Toonkel.
1st ed.
   p.   cm.
ISBN 1-55652-534-6
1. Househusbands.   2. Father and child.   3. Father and child—Case
studies.   4. Fathers—Psychology.   5. Child care.   6. Child rearing.
I. Toonkel, Jessica.   II. Title.
HQ756.6.B39 2004
306.874'2—dc22
2004007754

Cover design: Emily Brackett, Visible Logic
Cover photograph: The Image Bank/Regine Mahaux
Interior design: Pamela Juárez

Published by Chicago Review Press, Incorporated
814 North Franklin Street
Chicago, Illinois 60610
ISBN 1-55652-534-6
Printed in the United States of America
5 4 3 2 1

*This book is dedicated to my lovely wife, Sue,
and our two incredible boys, John and David*

*In loving memory of my parents, John and
Evangeline, who devoted their lives to family*

Contents

Acknowledgments

No project this large would be possible without the help of so many devoted fathers, colleagues, and friends. I am indebted to my first at-home dad friends, Dr. Bob Frank, Curtis Cooper, and Bruce Drobeck, who helped me early on with the *At-Home Dad Newsletter*; to Richard Axel, David Boylan, Chad Curtis, Chris Coby, Jim DiCenzo, Hogan Hilling, Peter Hoh, Marty Josephson, Steve Klem, Bill Laut, Hal Levy, Jay Massey, Bob Noonon, Barry Reszel, and Casey Spencer, all of whom joined me soon after; to the many more at-home dads with whom I have met over the years, who inspired me with their commitment to fatherhood; to Chris Stafford and Steve Harris, who paved the way before me; to Brian Basset, who graciously donated his wonderful *Adam@Home* cartoons to the *At-Home Dad Newsletter*, which led to this book; and to all the other dads not listed here who shared their stories and friendship with me.

I would also like to thank my oldest sister, Holly, who graciously provided her artwork to the *At-Home Dad Newsletter*; my youngest sister, Jeanne, who shared her generosity and recipes; my brother Chris, a veteran at-home dad to his son, Peter; my brother Charles, who always kept me in good spirits; my childhood friends Gerry Mroz, who provided me with my first computer, Frank Mroz, who gave me technical advice, and Rich Mroz and John Hinchey, who have recently started their own journeys as dads; my neighbors, John and Heidi Hood, for their commitment to family; fisherman Ken Donovan, who pulls me away from it all every year on his annual men's fishing weekend; Charles Bluman, who fought to keep me in journalism school when I needed him; those in the book whose names were changed for reasons of confidentiality; Jessica Toonkel, who got me started on the proposal and helped me through each chapter; my agent, Stacey Glick of Jane Dystel Literary Management, who tirelessly peddled the book proposal; Lisa Rosenthal of Chicago Review Press, for her final touches; and Cynthia Sherry of Chicago Review Press, who deserves the biggest thanks for taking on this book.

—Peter Baylies

I would like to thank my parents for their ongoing support of this project. Particularly, I would like to give special thanks to my mother, who always said I could write about anything and without whom this would not have been possible, and my husband, Maceo, who never got tired of hearing and reading about all the wonderful things that at-home dads do, and whom I know will be a spectacular father someday. More special thanks to my agent, Stacey Glick, for her constant words of encouragement and advice.

—Jessica Toonkel

Introduction

"Aather gooose," my then eighteen-month-old son, John, said to me impatiently. I thought he was just trying to get attention and continued to read the paper. He had been saying this for a few days and I didn't know what it meant. "AATHER GOOSE," he said, much louder now, bordering on a cry. After having been home with him for several months as an at-home dad, I knew that he was actually trying to say something, but I just wasn't able to understand his words yet.

"AATHER GOOSE!" John yelled, now in full hysterical mode. I scanned the house again for anything or anyone that might be called "aather goose." Then I got it. I proudly reached over to John's book pile, pulled off a book, and showed it to him. "*Mother Goose?*"

"NOOOOOO, AAAAATHER GOOSE!" he screamed, with tears streaming down his cheeks, his lips quivering, and his head shaking at how his own father could be so stupid. After taking a few deep breaths myself, I decided to try a new tactic and approach the situation as I would have dealt, just a few months earlier, with a difficult crybaby client. I got on the floor at his level. "What do you want?" I asked in as calm a manner as I could manage. After a few more "AATHER GOOSE" wails from my son and a few more wrong guesses on my part, the answer blurted out of me from the clear blue sky: "Is it *apple juice*?" My son suddenly stopped screaming and looked at me in silence with a smile.

This was my first real conversation with my son as an at-home dad.

This was also the moment I realized that being a stay-at-home dad would be filled with these episodes, and that these little interactions would teach us how to communicate with each other. While it is a never-ending succession of hurdles, it is also an ongoing reward as I continue to build relationships with my two sons in ways that would never be possible if I worked outside the house. And, after spending the last twelve years as a stay-at-home dad, I now know that it is these challenging moments and breakthroughs that show what being an at-home dad is all about.

During my first few months as a rookie stay-at-home dad, when my first son was closing in on his first birthday, I took many stroller walks around the block. I found plenty of moms pushing strollers, but no dads. I also saw little evidence of dads at the local playgrounds and shopping centers. I began to feel an uneasy sense of isolation. I needed some contact with anyone whose diaper I didn't have to change, even if it was just one dad I could talk with who was doing the same thing.

I decided to help myself, as well as other like-minded dads, so I sat down at my kitchen table during one of my son's three-hour naps and created the prototype for what would eventually become a quarterly publication called the *At-Home Dad Newsletter*. I thought about the most salient issues I faced in my new role: the isolation, my desire to connect with other dads to see if they were facing the same issues, the desire to save money and maybe even to run a home-based business. I began to look for other dads like myself, but instead of finding them on the playground, I finally found other dads on the Internet, hunched over their computers at home, desperately seeking comrades-in-arms via online chats and e-mail. I joined these online communities and started asking dads about their main concerns. The response was overwhelming, and many of them sent me their stories of why they became at-home dads and the issues they faced.

As the stories came pouring in, I heard tales of at-home dads dealing with comments such as, "So when will you be getting a real job?" or "Are you babysitting today?" Many also wished they could keep in touch with each other via e-mail or phone in order to start a local playgroup or to share their experiences of their home-based businesses. Others were worried about their finances and marriages. I found that many dads had solutions to other dads' problems, and I knew that with the newsletter I could bring these people together. With their stories, and a few of my own, I mailed the first issue of the *At-Home Dad Newsletter* to the media and six subscribers during the spring of 1994.

Ironically, the first mention of my newsletter was in *Woman's Day* magazine, shortly after my first issue came out, and just in time for Father's Day. Over time, as I gained readers, I found that a fair share of wives bought the newsletter for their husbands. A few wives commented to me that the reason they read the newsletter was because they "wanted to know what their husbands might be thinking."

As I published more issues, I found that many dads wanted to get together with other at-home dad families for social outings and playgroups for their kids. As a result, I started the At-Home Dad Network. The network started out as a list of dads from a few states and ended up including dads nationwide. The list has also expanded to provide names to the media and to researchers. (The At-Home Dad Network is provided free on the Web at www.at homedad.com.)

In 1995, after the newsletter had been going for a year, I got a call from Dr. Robert Frank of Glenview, Illinois, who was looking for dads to survey. Since I had the largest database of dads he could find, he and I decided to mail out 1,081 surveys to measure a number of issues, including isolation, income, daycare, and the level of satisfaction with staying at home. The number of completed responses we received—a total of 368 (34 percent response rate)—was the largest at-home dad survey of its kind ever done. (Throughout this book I will refer to the results of this study. See the resources section of this book for contact information for Dr. Frank.)

As my subscriber list grew, many national dailies and magazines, including *USA Today*, the *New York Times*, *Parents*, *Par-*

enting, and the *Christian Science Monitor*, began interviewing my readers and publishing their stories for a worldwide audience. The television and radio media soon followed, with my subscribers featured on *Oprah*, ABC's *Good Morning America*, CNN, and the BBC. With the publicity, the *At-Home Dad Newsletter* grew to become one of the first major resources for fathers who stayed at home to care for their children.

The speed at which the newsletter, and subsequently the online network, grew in popularity signaled to me that I was far from being alone. Before I knew it, I had more than a thousand readers. *The At-Home Dad Newletter* expanded to contain articles written for and by at-home dads, and it now regularly includes information from more than three hundred fathers, information about dozens of playgroups, and online message boards. I realized there was a need to aggregate all that I learned over the past ten years from the thousands of dads I met in person and online and to turn this accumulated knowledge into a comprehensive book.

Thus, I give you the *Stay-at-Home Dad Handbook*. In this book, I will share my own story about how I became an at-home dad and follow my personal journey with this often challenging, sometimes frustrating, but always joy-filled experience. There are many parenting books written by experts, and I am eternally grateful for their research. I have also found that dads who are in the frontlines of fatherhood are the real experts in parenting. So, in addition to my experiences, I hope you will enjoy the adventures and advice from other dads. In this book I will look at many aspects of being an at-home dad: transitioning to your first year at home, keeping your marriage healthy, connecting with other dads, living on one income, running your own business, housecleaning, suffering burnout, and deciding what to do when the kids start school. At the end of each chapter I share a Spotlight on Dad story that profiles a father and his experiences related to that chapter's topic. Also throughout the book, I have included Kid Tips for creative and fun games, along with some parenting ideas you can try with your kids. There is also an extensive resource listing in the back that provides additional sources of advice and inspiration. I hope that by the end of this book you will learn a few things that will help you on the wondrous journey of fatherhood. Just before the resources section, I've added more Spotlights on Dad to share the wisdom and experiences of a variety of at-home dads. Being an at-home dad isn't easy, but it's been the ride of my life! So, enjoy the book and have fun with your kids!

1

Starting Your New Career

A few weeks before Christmas 1992, my childcare provider called me at work with a worried tone in her voice. "I think your son has a fever," she said. "He won't stop crying. What should I do?" Just an hour after I'd dropped off my son at childcare, I found myself back in my car, rushing to pick him up. But as I reversed my dreaded one-hour commute, I secretly felt glad that, despite my son's illness, I had an excuse to spend a weekday with him.

During that drive, I began to daydream about what it would be like to stay home full time with my then nine-month-old son and how it would make my family's life so much easier, since we wouldn't have the rush-rush lifestyle of two working parents. This was an idea that I liked to think about a lot, but since I didn't think we could pull it off financially, I didn't have the nerve to quit my job.

John was born the previous March; my wife, Sue, a schoolteacher, had stayed home with him, right through her summer vacation. My boss allowed me to stay home for a week with my baby, which was about par for many dads at the time in the corporate world. (The Family and Medical Leave Act, which would have allowed me up to twelve weeks to care for my son, didn't exist yet. It wasn't signed into law by President Bill Clinton until August 1993.)

That fall, we were lucky enough to find an excellent daycare center on our street. Like many of our friends, we found ourselves living the day-to-day dual income lifestyle. Each morning, I would drop John off at daycare at 7:30, the beginning of my commute to work. Although my son was in good hands, my wife would be worried sick because, in a group of six other children, she feared he wasn't getting the one-on-one attention that she could give him. An entry in my wife's journal, written for John to read someday, was telling: September 22, 1992: "I wish I could be with you every second of the day and protect you. All these ear infections, colds, fears—You are so young for it all. . . . I miss the time with you." She could hardly wait to pick him up at four o'clock each weekday.

My wife's anxiety led us to discuss the possibility of her staying home with John, but I feared that the layoffs at my computer company might catch up with me.

On a Friday afternoon in December, one of the many waves of layoffs that swept through my company finally captured me in its wake. My boss informed me that I was "involuntarily terminated." As I sat there in shock, wondering what the future would hold, anxious at how we would make ends meet, I was secretly relieved and happy. My wish to stay home with John had come true. It was the best Christmas present I'd ever received from a boss! I finally had my son on a full-time basis.

This chapter will give you a first taste of what it will be like to be an at-home dad and will provide an introduction to the challenges you'll face.

Making the Decision

Whether you decide to be the primary caregiver voluntarily or as a result of circumstance, the new role will take you by surprise. It will change your life just as your decision to get married or have a child did, and like those events, it will come with many joys and disappointments. Peter Steinberg of Springfield, Virginia, started making his decision during the many chats he had with his kids' preschool teacher, who supported the idea. "She had a big influence on us, and it got my wife and me talking seriously about it," he says. When his oldest child asked why he worked, the only thing he could say was, "So I can pay for daycare for you." Then a defining moment came that made him quit.

> One time when I went to pick my son up at preschool, there was a very bad car accident. It usually takes thirty minutes to get to daycare, but this time it took three hours. When I finally got there, my son was watching the news instead of Barney, and said to me, "Daddy, I thought you would never pick me up."

Add to that the fact that his wife, Caroline, made more money, and the decision to stay home was pretty clear.

Timothy Nohe of Catonville, Maryland, who cares for three children, says,

> I quit my electrical engineering job eighteen months ago and haven't looked back. I hated that job. All government work and programming. Yuck! We had a seventeen-year-old daughter, a five-year-old son, and a six-month-old son we had adopted as an infant. The baby was in daycare. My wife made more than 60 percent of our household income. More than half of my share went to daycare and before and after care. What's wrong with this picture?

Brian Rollins of Dayton, Ohio, says his main reason for becoming a stay-at-home dad was simply to be there for his kids:

> My own instinct before I started being an at-home dad (five years ago) was that young children needed a parent to be there for them at all times. Day in and day out I have been

there for my three sons. We've spent long, lazy days roaming the local park and throwing rocks in the "little river." We've ridden the city bus and explored downtown with all the glass buildings and old-fashioned elevators. We've spent hours just snuggling together on the couch and watching silly kids shows. (Yep, TV is probably not a good thing, but the closeness we feel for each other during those times is one of my most precious memories.) I've learned about my own feelings toward my kids and gotten to know them better than just about anybody else on the planet. In turn, my kids have learned about who I really am. It has been a good experience for all of us.

No! No! NO!

When my two-year-old son, John, wants to go outside, he comes to me and says, "Outside! Outside! Outside! Outside! Outside! Outside! Outside!" (in that order). What to do when it's raining, or it's just not a good time to go outside? Instead of answering his pleas with, "No! No! NO!" I looked him straight in the eye one day and said in a low but firm voice, "Do you know why you cannot go outside, John? Because it's raining out, that's why!" He stopped and actually started listening. Seizing the moment, I then said, "Now tell Daddy why you can't go outside." He stopped, wiped his tears, and answered back, "Because it's raining?" I've used this technique ever since. I found that as long as he gets an answer as to why he can't do something, he usually stops asking and goes on to another project.

—*From the Author*

Stories such as those of these men fit the results of researcher Dr. Robert Frank, who conducted a survey of 368 readers of the *At-Home Dad Newsletter*. Dr. Frank found that the main reason dads stayed home is to keep their kids out of daycare.

Many dads are not fortunate enough to choose to stay at home with their kids, and instead find themselves in this role due to a tough economy. More and more men are taking on the role of primary caregiver simply because they cannot find a job. When I lost my job, I seized the opportunity to be an at-home dad, but many fathers do not. For these dads, who are making the change not by choice but by necessity, the adjustment may be more challenging, and at times, unbearable.

Whether you are considering becoming an at-home dad by choice or this role is thrust upon you, there are a number of important issues to discuss with your partner that will help you make an informed decision. It's important to be honest and open during this discussion and also to be a good listener. Here are some issues you'll need to discuss to figure out how this choice will affect your household financially and emotionally:

- What are your fixed expenses?
- What are your variable expenses?
- Can you meet all of these needs on one income?
- What does daycare cost?
- How much will you automatically save by being at home (daycare, car expenses, work clothes)?
- Are there ways you can cut down on expenses to make it possible to survive on just one income?
- What are the benefits of this choice in terms of cooking, and thus of saving money by eating out less?
- How will the loss of a second income affect your family's entertainment?
- Will family vacations still be possible?

- Can you afford to hire a babysitter and go out on a date without the kid(s)?
- Are you the kind of person who can stay home during the day?
- What are the long-term benefits to your children and wife?

There are many more issues to discuss, but this list will give you a good head start.

The First Days

Since it was Christmastime when I was laid off, and Sue was off on her school's Christmas break, too, I had the luxury to treat my first days as an at-home dad like a vacation. My vacation ended the day she returned to work. That's the day being an at-home dad officially became my new career. As the winter days got colder, my new life jarred me out of my cubicle-induced autopilot lifestyle and into a fresh routine that unpredictably changed with my growing baby. Each morning, with Sue off to school at seven o'clock, John would eventually wake up and I would change him, feed him, and play games with him. Compared to my old job as a software engineer, this was a job that required a full day of attention. My trips to the watercooler at work were replaced by trips to the baby wipes. Instead of "doing" lunch, I was spooning cereal with yogurt into John. Instead of meeting with my coworkers, I was meeting with my son's pediatrician.

After I spent one week as a rookie at-home dad, my wife made the following entry in her journal written for John:

You and your dad had your first full week together. You weren't feeling great with the cough and all, but things went well, it seems. Dad loves getting to really know you, your moods, the subtle signals you give. You're getting to be great buddies.

I would play with John, read to him, and take care of his needs while my wife prepared dinner. I was amazed that the simplest things would amuse him. I remember I used to put my hand just below the edge of the table and pop it up to make him laugh. He kept following my hand to see where it would jump up next. (Now that he is twelve, this doesn't seem to work anymore, but it doesn't stop me.) Times like this made me relish being home with him all the more. Getting a huge grin from my son was a lot more rewarding than a flattering e-mail from my boss.

The transition period to adjust to my new role lasted about six months, but it can take much longer, depending on how drastic the change is for you, your experience with children, and how many kids you will be caring for at one time. (You and your wife should set a reasonable span of time for a trial run to stay home with your children, keeping in mind that you need to give yourself six months to a year, not just a few weeks, to adjust to your new role.) For me, beginning my new life during the New England winter made it harder. When Mother Nature treated us to many subzero days, I was housebound with an infant. The walls began to close in on me.

I learned a lot of hard lessons in my first days as an at-home dad. These lessons, which I will examine throughout this book, include:

- Being an at-home dad includes household chores as well as childcare. Unless your name is Trump.
- Dishes need to be washed. Dishes, once dirty, don't disappear on their own. Either they have to be put in the dishwasher (and the dishwasher turned on and then emptied) or you need to start using paper plates whenever possible if you want to cut down on your dish-

washing duty. And baby food doesn't sit too well on paper.

- Create an environment that your wife will enjoy coming home to, even if you don't care if the house is a little messy. By cleaning, you will make your wife happy—so if you don't want to clean for yourself, do it for your wife. (See Chapter 3 for more on housecleaning.)
- Remember that your wife worked hard all day, too. Give her a pat on the back, even when she doesn't have one for you. (See Chapter 2 for a discussion of the tensions this situation can create.)
- Related to this, sometimes you must give yourself a sorely needed pat on the back for a job well done.

Losing Your Status as Breadwinner

In addition to juggling the diaper changes with the dishwashing and housekeeping duties, you need to grow comfortable with the idea that you are no longer a breadwinner. This can be incredibly freeing, but it can also be terrifying. When one dad decided to stay at home with his daughter, he began to have second thoughts. "The stress of the decision was unreal," he says. The question he had to ask himself was: "Can I live with myself if I forego the precious time with my daughter to earn this income?" Ask yourself this question, and if your answer is no, then the monetary adjustments, while difficult at times, will be worth it.

Once you and your wife have made the decision for you to stay home with the kids, the next thing you need to do is figure out your new budget. Obviously, putting some money away before you quit your current job is preferable, but many at-home dads do not have this luxury. When I left my job and figured out my budget, I found that by the time I deducted daycare, gas, car repairs, lunches, clothes, and more, I wasn't making half as much as I thought. As for the other half I did make, it just wasn't worth the time. (See Chapter 5 for tips on living on one income.)

Also, just because you are quitting your current job to stay at home with your kids does not mean that you can't still make money. Many at-home dads with whom I have spoken over the years have found that they can start home businesses and end up making more money than they were making when working for someone else. (I will discuss this further in Chapter 6.)

When I was the breadwinner of the family, I received a concrete result for my labor: a paycheck. But suddenly my wife was the sole income-earner. This didn't bother me as long as we could make it with one income. Jim Mains of Oak Park, Illinois, notes that when his wife became the breadwinner of the family, he had trouble buying her a gift:

> What am I going to do, buy her $40 worth of roses with her money? I needed to realize that my working wife most likely would not come home each evening and shower me with affection and thank yous for being the perfect father and husband. Instead of a boss giving me a monthly job performance report, my kids were busy giving me a minute-by-minute performance report in the form of tears or smiles.

Candlelight Dinners for Kids

Kids keep popping out of their seats during dinner? Keep the focus with a candle in the middle of the table and the lights off. You will find that the kids will be less distracted and will keep their eyes and mind on the family and food (since that's all they will see!). If your kids are young, keep the candle out of reach.

—*Susan Baylies, North Andover, Massachusetts*

Being able to feel like you contribute to your family's well-being is important. Perhaps factoring a discretionary budget into your larger household budget will help you make the transition.

Mr. Mom

Another challenge for at-home dads is how people react to the fact that they are the primary caregivers. Whether friends, family, or complete strangers, everyone has two cents to lend about what you are doing. As we said above, many people still expect the husband to be the breadwinner and the wife to be the nurturer, and when these roles are reversed, people often stick their noses up in judgment. As one dad puts it, "Even the man I can most complimentarily term the town drunk has a viewpoint. One day he lurched up into my face and growled, 'F'cripes sake, why don't you get a real job?'"

When I made the choice to be an at-home dad, I felt the added pressure of needing to prove to one of my sisters that I could pull it off. She made bets on how long it would take me to decide to return to work.

One particularly irritated at-home dad decided to just start telling people his hobbies, letting them believe that it was part of his job at home. "I got so good that when I was done responding to their question, they were green with envy: home all day, work when I want, and have money to buy my toys (my wife gives me a generous allowance)." However, once people caught on that he did not have a real job, their attitudes toward him changed. "Strange that such a trivial matter could influence a directly opposite response in a person."

Among the various negative comments that at-home dads hear from people, the one they find the most annoying is being called Mr. Mom—a term that comes from the 1983 movie with Michael Keaton and Teri Garr. Even though it is more than twenty years later, this label seems to have stuck. Most dads I talk to find that

Creative Pancakes

Next time you make pancakes, get creative and make eating more fun. Pour two round "ears" on the top and you've got a Mickey Mouse pancake! My son came up with the idea to use the butter for eyes, nose, and mouth! Another favorite is my Milky Way pancake. Just pour a small pancake and then slowly drip circles around it to form the galaxy. Or make pizza pancakes by cutting pancakes into slices just like a pizza.

—From the Author

humor is the most effective way to thwart negative comments. Not only does it make you feel better, but it may help others see the absurdity of the comments they make.

A good tactic to take with negative comments is to turn them around. When John Daniels, from Portland, Oregon, was asked how he could afford to stay at home, he replied, "I can't afford not to stay at home." Responses such as this demonstrate that you take your job seriously, because being an at-home dad is a real job. If the comments come from strangers and it is obvious that they are trying to make you feel bad about what you are doing, then walk away. You aren't going to be able to change their minds. While comments such as "Are you babysitting today?" or "When are you going to get a real job?" are frustrating because they seem to undermine what you are doing, you need to be able to keep it in perspective. In the end, the only people who you should be trying to impress are yourself and your family. When dads stay at home with their kids, it can have a more positive effect on their children, which is the most important factor of all. Dr. Frank found that children have a more equal relationship with both parents when the father stays home with them. He says,

With fathers at home and mothers working, we see a more equal balance of parenting. The father spends most of the day with the child and the mother spends the evening with the child. The child feels the attention of two parents to a greater extent than [in] the traditional family where the child sees a lot [more] of the mother and not the father. Both parents are more involved in the child's life, and this has great benefits for the child.

Now that I have been home for the last twelve years, I know that I have given and will continue to give my family the best upbringing that I can offer. Since I am confident about my role at home, I am not bothered by any "get a real job" comments, which can be hard to shake for some. Remember, take the comments with humor and remember what really matters—your children.

Indeed, I have spoken to many rookie at-home dads who get so caught up with proving themselves to everyone that they lose sight of their children. Focusing on your kids is essential during the first few months as a stay-at-home dad. John Stephens of Champaign, Illinois, realized what he was missing.

I hadn't yet recognized the magnificent fortune I had to be able to spend such valuable time with my son. I was looking at our time together as a chore, rather than a chance to give my son a good upbringing, one where we could learn so much from each other.

With time and patience, you, too, can have this revelation.

Isolation Creeps In

So your wife has gone back to work, and you have been an at-home dad for several weeks. While you are constantly busy running around, doing chores, and watching the kids, you know you are learning and improving your ability to do this job. But you may start realizing how little you are interacting with other adults. When you do see adults, they are mostly older than you (retirees) and mothers, whether it's at the playground or the supermarket. Not seeing other dads can make you feel even more out of place.

Many stay-at-home dads I know say that isolation is the hardest thing to conquer during the first few months of being at home with the kids. Dr. Frank's survey results also found that 63 percent of at-home dads reported they were "somewhat isolated," while 6 percent said they were "totally isolated." One dad from California who had been home with his two young sons says, "The hardest part is not knowing anyone, plus everyone else is at work all day. After talking to a three-year-old all day, I can't wait for my wife to get home."

Part of this initial feeling of isolation comes from a loss of identity. Without an outside career to define yourself, you are no longer sure what you want or who you are. You will now be defined more as a family man and father than how your peers viewed you before you had kids. Many fathers use this feeling of not being a separate self as an inspiration to start over and go back to things they used to enjoy when they were younger, in their pre-career days. John Stephens realized how important it was to set aside time for himself during the first few months of being at home with his son.

> I decided I had to start doing something for myself. I'd stopped doing the things I'd done earlier to give myself moments of serenity, such as writing and painting. Things that give us a sense of self-worth outside of caring for our family are extremely important. Without them, we begin to lose our sense of identity.

Think about what you used to do and try to take at least thirty minutes a day to do that. Maybe you can do this during naptime if you have young children at home. It doesn't matter if the kitchen is filled with dishes or if dinner will be a little late. It is important to take that time just to nourish and refresh yourself. This will also keep you from feeling as if you are taking care of everyone else's needs but not your own.

Finding Other Dads

Another major complaint I hear from at-home dads making the transition is that they can't find other, like-minded dads. This was a very depressing reality for me when I started. What I soon realized is that many dads don't reach out to each other as much as at-home moms do. Just as we don't like to ask other people for directions, we are even more reluctant to ask each other how to keep babies from crying when the television isn't on, or how long to let them nap in the afternoon so they will still go to sleep at a reasonable hour. And maybe we don't reach out to other dads because we think that if we try to meet other at-home dads, we will only talk about those kinds of things, and not manly things such as last night's football game, like we used to do with our coworkers. We are hesitant because we are worried that the others may perceive us as wimps. I remember a few years ago I attended the annual At-Home Dads Convention in Chicago, and began talking to *Esquire*'s contributing editor, Ted Allen. We had a pleasant conversation about putting nearly naked women on the cover of publications in order to sell more issues to men. He then paused, looked around, and noted, "Gee, you seem to be a strong, well-put-together guy. I thought you and the other guys would be soft and wimpy." The fact is we all want to find each other, but we let our egos prevent us from reaching out.

This was a big issue for me when I started out at home, and I turned to the Internet for help by starting the At-Home Dad Network—an online community for fathers. This network has since turned into dozens of playgroups across the country, since dads find that organizing these sessions with their kids is the best way to meet each other. Going online or to your kids' schools and starting or finding a playgroup (whether it's dads-only or not) is one way to find other men like yourself. (In Chapter 4 I'll discuss the details of how to start a dad's playgroup and other ways to make connections.)

I have heard dads compare their experiences of becoming at-home dads with their own children's experiences of starting school—it's about making friends all over again in a different context.

Establishing a Routine

I can't count the number of times new at-home dads have told me how they thought their new lives were going to be so much calmer, with more time on their hands, since they would be home all day.

Role-Playing Stories

My daughter, Liza, and I tell each other what we have come to call "baby stories." It gives me the perfect opportunity to practice my storytelling technique, and it inspires my daughter to remember details and practice her storytelling skill as well. I begin by telling Liza (age six) a story from her infant years. It always involves her, and it usually has to do with some dramatic event that her mother and I will never forget. I stick to the truth, but I provide as many descriptive details as I can recall and make it as interesting to Liza as possible. It doesn't seem to matter to Liza that I tell some of the same stories over and over again. Then it is Liza's turn. I ask her to tell me a story about her that I would not otherwise know. It might be an event from her years in daycare or something that happened while she was with a babysitter. I encourage her to recall colors, smells, emotional responses, and more. The result is usually a story that she enjoys telling more than once! Such storytelling skills will serve our children well as they begin taking creative writing courses in school.

—*Dan Dunsmore, Charlottesville, Virginia*

When you were working and someone else was home with your kids or your kids were at daycare, the daily care of the children and home was "out of sight, out of mind." However, when it's you getting the kids dressed, feeding them, and keeping them entertained most of the day, on top of doing the housecleaning and grocery shopping and making dinner, you will be more exhausted than you ever thought you could be. As one father puts it, "Let's lay it on the line: If your child were your boss, you'd quit."

Be prepared to be overwhelmed for the first few months as you figure out how to balance your various new roles. Establish a new routine to give your day structure. Even the simplest things, such as driving your wife to work or getting lunches together at the same time once or twice a week, will establish a schedule that you can start to work around. This new routine will keep your day a little more predictable for you and your kids.

Other dads have found many solutions that helped create more structure in the home:

- Use a planner to keep life organized.
- Join the YMCA or any other kid-friendly organization.
- Give yourself "daddy breaks" at naptime and work at your own hobbies.
- If you want to further your schooling, start an online master's degree program in which you can go at your own pace.
- Make a to-do list for the minor repairs in and out of the house, and try to do at least one a day.
- If your kids are in school, volunteer in your kids' classes a few hours a week or more.
- Set an exercise regime for yourself—working out not only will help you get rid of anxiety, frustration, and stress, it will also give you some time with yourself. Many gyms have daycare facilities.

There are other ways to establish a routine that makes daily life easier to manage. One dad even took in another child four days a week as a playmate before his second child was born. "That kept me busy and then established a new routine with its own sense of structure." Another dad reports, "I set up a home schedule of chores, activities, and errands. Laundry is done two days a week, cooking for supper starts at 4:30 every day. Fun activities are spaced out throughout the week, and family time is Friday night."

In general, setting goals for yourself can help you get through the day. Whether it's fixing up a part of the house, losing weight, learning a new skill, or teaching your children how to do something, it can help you break up the time. Set daily as well as weekly and monthly goals, since some activities, such as painting a room, take longer to complete. Try to update your goals every three to six months—this way you are constantly working toward new things. This will also help you make adjustments with the changing needs of your children as they grow.

Having a weekly family time is a great idea for a routine. A simple one we use is every Friday night is pizza night—no cleanup! Structure can even come about in the form of a weekly game for the kids. Our family now plays a game called Family Jeopardy. This is an idea I got from my neighbors, John and Heidi Hood. Every Monday night one of their four children prepares twenty-five questions about the family or current events. Then that kid poses the questions to the rest of the family, giving out points for the first correct answer. They play this with uncles and aunts and even sometimes other neighbors. Just watching the kids decide who pressed the "buzzer" first is half the fun. This game ends up being a routine that creates an entertaining way to build structure around the home and connection among family members.

Making sure that each member of the family has a routine task to help with at dinnertime is another way to create structure, and it can keep a very hectic time, such as when your wife comes home from work, manageable. Have the kids do simple things such as setting the table or cutting vegetables (for the older ones). If they aren't old enough for that, maybe you can have them make flowers out of paper or draw pictures to use as table centerpieces. This will also free you up to get dinner done.

And Then There Were Two

With my first son, my toughest transition was learning how to slow down to his pace. What at first seemed like a boring hour of sitting on the floor with my child actually became the happiest moments we spent together. On May 4, 1995, after 2½ years of staying home with my son John (who was then three), we added another son, David, to our family. Deciding to have another child was easy, since my wife and I loved having one and knew a second would be twice as fun and would provide a ready playmate for John. Caring for my two sons has truly become my career. I realized the more I got to know my kids, the more I looked forward to being with them.

Here are a few tips to help you prepare for a second (or third, or fourth . . .) child:

- Remember that you may need to re-childproof the house: recheck the electrical plugs and spaces the little ones should not get into.
- You will have less time for yourself and your wife; try to plan free time for both of you.
- Don't let yourself or your wife get too tired; give each other breaks at night. You will need the energy for the nightly wake-ups.
- Don't forget to give your older children attention so that they don't feel left out of the excitement.
- Give your older children some small chores to help out with the baby, such as getting the baby bottle and retrieving the diapers for Dad to change, thus allowing

them to play an important role (and therefore build a sense of responsibility) in their sibling's life!

- And finally, if you were home for the first child or children, allow yourself to relax a little. You figured out how to take care of them the first go-round. This may help you think of tasks with a little more ease and less stress.

I hope this chapter has helped give you a general idea of what to expect in your rookie year as an at-home dad. With a little effort, you will overcome any feelings of isolation you may have and build your confidence in your new role. The first few years can be hectic for you and your wife. In the next chapter, I will look closely at the problems your marriage may encounter in your new at-home dad family.

SPOTLIGHT ON DAD
"A Personal Diary"

BY DAN DUNSMORE   *Dan Dunsmore lives in Charlottesville, Virginia. Here he talks about his first days as an at-home dad.*

Wednesday, September 29. I had been a teacher for fourteen years, three weeks, and three days. My five-year-old daughter had just begun attending the same school where I had been teaching, and I was on my way to pick her up on the lower-school campus. I felt as if I had just been released from a cage—ready to fly but not sure in which direction. When I met Liza in front of her classroom, and she said, "This is the last day of being here all day long!" I smiled and told her I wanted to take the long way home since it was such a sunny day and we could see the airplanes at the airport. She screamed, "No, Daddy, no! I want to go straight home and watch a movie." Thus began my first afternoon as a stay-at-home dad.

I spot-cleaned the house, but there was no pattern to the cleaning. Spot-cleaning the house in the afternoons after picking up Liza from daycare or school was something I had done for the past five years. It had provided a momentary escape from thinking about teaching, and cleared the clutter from the evening before and that morning. I hate clutter! Liza and I then played a game or two, but as soon as Tory (Liza's friend) came home, Liza went next door to play for at least an hour. I sat on the couch and thought, "So this is the way it's going to be."

Thursday, September 30. Kim, my wife of twelve years, turned off the alarm and made her way sleepily to the shower. I rushed to the kitchen to make a pot of coffee. She had said a week earlier, "You don't have to wake up with me. It'd be nice, but you don't have to." I said, "But I want to. I want this move to mean more time for us, too." The conversation that Kim, Liza, and I had this morning was pleasant—a far cry from the hectic breakfasts of the past three and a half weeks. Those had usually included demands that Liza eat three more bites and that she had to wear socks to go to school. She would answer our demands by falling on the floor and screaming, "I don't want to go to school." On the way to school, she said out of nowhere, "I loved today!" I asked why. (Liza has always known which buttons to push.) "Because I got to be home with you, Daddy." I spent the afternoon at the post office and the grocery store. I looked for other men who might be buying stamps or groceries on a Thursday afternoon, but I saw only one or two. Tears came to my eyes, and I asked myself for the first time, "What the hell have I done?"

Friday, October 1. God, I felt great! No papers to grade, no smartass students, no planning for class. This afternoon I cleaned some more. I can't believe I already feel just a bit restless.

Saturday, October 2. I took Liza to ballet. Her class met in an old church sanctuary. The morning sun filtered in to give the room a warm, Spielbergian glow. Again I found myself counting the number of men who accompanied their little girls to ballet, and I was impressed with the large number of attentive dads. I was also scared to death that one of them, or even a mother, might casually ask what I do for a living. I've been experimenting with some answers. "I'm a househusband." "I'm unemployed." "I'm a writer." "I'm a former teacher."

Sunday, October 3. Tonight I helped Liza with her bath, washed her hair, and watched the last part of a movie. There were no tears, no shouts, no anxiety caused by rushing Liza to bed. Still I didn't feel totally relaxed until I began writing a couple of short stories that had been floating around my head. I was doing something that I considered creatively stimulating for the first time in days.

Monday, October 4. Kim called and asked if Liza and I could have lunch with her before I took Liza to school. It was a great idea, and the very sort of thing we could never do if I were teaching.

Tuesday, October 5. The more I'm out in public and no one asks why I'm not at work, the better I feel. Of course, strangers never asked me that in the summertime. Why would they ask me now? I went by the library to find a how-to book on publishing. I noticed several women with their children, a few adults obviously doing research, and a couple of men reading magazines. Are they also at-home dads? Am I the only man in the world doing this? I do feel isolated right now. . . . I think I'm mainly just scared. For the first time in my life, I'm not sure what is going to happen next. I know Kim will go to work and Liza will go to school, but what will I do? Is being a stay-at-home dad enough? Will I teach again? Will I ever work outside the home again?

Wednesday, October 6. I called my brother-in-law's wife, Jennifer, to ask how she handled being a full-time, stay-at-home mom. She was very helpful, too. I even talked to a local social worker to see if there were some local, statewide, or nationwide support groups for stay-at-home dads. There were none that he knew of, but he found the idea fascinating.

Thursday, October 7. I chased Liza around the furniture in the living room a few days ago. Now she wants me to do that each morning. So we did it at least half a dozen times. After school we stopped off at another park and played for at least an hour. I felt great! There were several other children at the park who were being watched by several au pairs. A retired couple got the biggest kick out of Liza's interaction with me.

Sunday, October 10. Liza walked quietly into the living room and said, "Daddy, can I sleep in here with you? I'm having dreams about witches and dragons." We curled up together on the couch. I hadn't felt this at peace with myself for months.

Monday, October 11. I've become painfully aware of every extra dollar I've spent recently. Something's wrong with one of our cars. This also worries me. Liza and I stopped by the neighborhood park to play this afternoon. I was a little on edge, but Liza enjoyed herself. She and I worked a difficult puzzle together several times before dinner. We were both relaxed, not rushed at all. This feeling of not being rushed is strange and awkward to me. Liza soaked in the tub this evening for at least thirty minutes. She loved it and I didn't feel rushed to remove her, screaming, from the water so that I could quickly comb her hair while she squirmed—which, in the past, I might eventually answer with a pop on her naked bottom. Ah! This is why I stopped teaching—no screaming, no squirming, and no pop on the bottom to punctuate the end of another tense, hectic day.

2

At-Home Dads and Marriage: When the Rush Hour Starts at Home

When I started as an at-home dad, I simply neglected the basic tasks around the house, and my wife would instinctively take over when she got home, cooking the dinner and doing most of the cleaning and laundry. It was the same routine we both had when I was working. I didn't even think of it, and in the beginning, neither did Sue. She had grown up on a farm in Ohio and was cooking a full meal by the time she was nine. I grew up in the suburbs of Boston and spent most of my time riding my Stingray bike around the neighborhood, waiting for my mom to ring the dinner bell. My mom did all the cooking and cleaning while my dad worked. Now, several decades later, I was behaving just as my dad did, except I didn't have an outside job. As the months passed, my wife grew more tired and frustrated because she continued to manage the roles of breadwinner, housekeeper, and cook, while I was home more of the time but not contributing much more than I had before. She grew upset that the house was not cleaned on a regular basis. To make things worse, being the procrastinator that I am, I would wait until a few minutes before she'd get home before frantically skim-cleaning the kitchen. I came to realize that my wife was managing these chores, which should have now been mine because of my increased time at home.

In this chapter I will take a close look at the problems your marriage might face as you become an at-home dad, and I'll offer some solutions. I will look at the hectic period between when your kids come home from school and your wife comes home from work. I'll also offer stories from dads who have wives that work late hours. Stories from other dads will show you how to simplify the dinner hour and keep a smooth bedtime routine. Finally, I will explore and provide solutions to the lack of intimacy cause by hectic schedules and a lack of communication.

Hell Hour

For most dads, the period between when your kids come home from school and your wife comes home from work are the hours that can make or break you. This scene may already be familiar to you. Hell descends between 5 and 7 P.M., but you are oblivious to the time. One of your kids has the television turned up all the way as he sits transfixed, playing his video game, while the younger one is running around the house trying to escape the fate of having to brush his teeth. While chasing him, you try to put a pillow back here, throw some toys to the side there, but cleaning the house is pointless at this stage. The smell of something resembling burning rubber is wafting through the house, and by the time you realize that smell was supposed to be dinner, it's too late. That's when you hear the car door slam and the front door open, and your tired and frustrated wife walks in, assesses the scene, and sighs deeply. This is the time that many dads refer to as hell hour.

Roland LaScala of Wooster, Ohio, recalls,

> My wife came home shortly before 7 P.M. dragging from a cold after another stressful day, of which there have been many lately. The kids were just finishing eating because I

stalled dinner to wait for my wife and then gave up and fed them, another common occurrence. She needed to crawl into bed, but instead sat on the couch in the family room like a zombie, and the kids were all over her screaming. I got protective of her and yelled at the kids and then felt guilty that I yelled at them.

One major threat to any at-home dad's marriage happens around this time of day. Just when you need to unwind from your day, your wife is also ready to relax. When you both have a long day and you meet at the door without a game plan, the results are often disastrous.

Josh Collins of Charlotte, Virginia, who works four evenings a week as a part-time tech support representative, gets his evening routine thrown off if his wife arrives home late.

I get a little irritated if Judy gets home after 4:30 because I usually need help occupying (or supervising) four-year-old Caitlin and three-month-old Kevin while dinner is prepared. If Judy is home late, dinner can be late, which makes getting to work more stressful. However, if Judy is home early, I get an unexpected break that helps me unwind before having to dash out.

This routine gets old quick. Everyone feels taken for granted, frustrations will arise, and resentments will grow if you don't change the situation.

Creating a Game Plan

Like many at-home dads and their working wives, Sue and I quickly realized that we needed a game plan. We sat down and worked out a new routine in which I would pick up a higher percentage of the laundry, cooking, and housecleaning duties. I ended up doing the cooking during the weekdays, with my wife doing it on Saturday and Sunday. I have also promised to keep the house clean and a meal ready (or nearly ready) when my wife comes in the door after work.

Remember that your wife may be coming from the quiet environment of an office job into the shock of a home filled with screaming kids, so it's a good idea to factor in some time for her to decompress. You may be surprised, especially if you have a few toddlers, at how loud and annoying they can be—even when they are simply playing—if you are entering their space from a quiet time and place.

If you have more than one child, talk to your wife about dividing the children between the two of you when she first gets home. Roland LaScala found that this strategy worked for his family:

> On normal days, my wife is walking through the door and I am trying to get dinner on the table. Generally she will have one of the kids come with her into the bedroom while she gets changed and I will have the other help me set the table. That's her way of relieving me at the worst time of the day.

However, if you are going to do this, make sure the kids don't feel as if they are just being passed off. Karl Ochsner of Scottsdale,

Crabby Hat

Here's a unique solution when your patience wears thin from time to time. I have a floppy hat with crabs on it. I call it my crabby hat. When I have the hat on, the kids know to change their behavior.

—*Mike Becker, Naperville, Illinois*

Arizona, recalls a friend who passes his children off the minute his wife comes through the door:

> This is very unfair to both parties. The kids are not a ping-pong ball. My wife's workday takes a toll on her too. In our household, my daughter is at the stage where she wants me to do everything, take her to the potty, get her dressed, etc., where it takes a toll on giving me any freedom.

At-Home Dad Contract

Peter and Caroline Steinberg of Springfield, Virginia, came up with a unique but effective way to make their first year easier by creating a contract of what they expected of each other. Caroline says, "When we sat down and drew up the contract, it forced us to think of how we value the household chores and duties. We ended up talking it all out that night and it worked great." Peter adds, "It didn't turn into an argument, it made us think of the things I do anyway."

On the following page is part of the contract the Steinbergs drew up. If you would like to prevent a ton of arguments, you may want to try this out. Using the Steinbergs' contract as a guide, sit down with your wife, figure out the duties and responsibilities around your house, divide them equitably, and then honor your contract.

While this contract might be taking matters to the extreme, it should serve as a good template for the kinds of issues and responsibilities you both need to address with each other before you take the leap to become a stay-at-home dad. Using this contract as a guide, figure out the duties and responsibilities that are needed to make your family life as stress-free as possible. Identifying the household responsibilities and assessing your expectations at the beginning is a great way to start out on the right foot.

At-Home Dad Contract

The said purpose of this contract is to specify the roles and expectations of _____ (husband) and _____ (wife) while _____ (husband) acts as the primary caregiver of their children and _____ (wife) acts as the primary moneymaker. Both parties reserve the right to discuss any changes to this agreement by calling a family meeting. Both parties agree that this contract will be evaluated every six months while _____ is a stay-at-home dad.

_____ (husband) will carry out the following functions:

- Get girls dressed, make them lunch, and take them to school
- Handle doctor appointments and attend to girls when they are sick
- Make sure the girls are involved with playgroups and outside activities
- Pay the bills and balance the checkbook
- Take care of the outside of the house and hire contractors when needed
- Do a majority of the grocery shopping and errands
- Do the laundry and fold it when done
- Be responsible for trash collection
- Cook dinner five to six nights a week and clean up dinner while _____ (wife) attends to the girls

_____ (wife) will carry out the following functions:

- Be the primary moneymaker of the family
- Pick out the girls' clothes in the morning
- Oversee bedtime routines on weeknights
- Be responsible for dinner one to two nights per week
- Do the taxes

Roles and Expectations of Being a Couple

- _____ (husband) will be allowed to go out with the guys once a month
- _____ (wife) will be allowed to go out with the girls once a month
- _____ (husband) and _____ (wife) will do their best to go out as a couple at least once a month
- support each other in decisions made on behalf of the girls

By signing below, _____ (husband) and _____ (wife) are entering into this contract on the _____ day of this month _____ in the year 20_____.

_____   _____
(husband)   Date

_____   _____
(wife)   Date

Family Meetings

When making the transition to becoming an at-home dad, working together may require more effort than a traditional family. Many families, such as the Steinbergs, use family meetings as a way to communicate regularly with each other and discuss any issues that arise. For families with kids who are old enough, family meetings are a great opportunity to include your children and hear what they have to say, too. This is a good time to help clear the air on some issues that may be bothering them and to allow them to feel as if they are being heard. Mike Kennedy of Aurora, Illinois, finds the meetings really help his family.

> My wife and I will state what the problem is and ways we can solve it. The children really enjoy putting their two cents in for problem resolution. Most of the time, my wife and I have the final word.

Family meetings are also a good time to catch up with each other and make sure you are all doing your stated roles. You can have one each month to keep all family members up to date and communicating, and you can schedule emergency meetings when serious issues arise.

Simplifying Dinnertime

Once you both have sat down and worked out the details of how you would ideally like this arrangement to work, you will need to get the kids adjusted to the game plan. In order to get daily life to run smoothly, set a routine that the kids become familiar with, and that will be simple to follow. In time, you may even get a few extra minutes with your wife to enjoy each other's company. The bottom line is: simplicity is the key. And the first step to making your life easier is to simplify the dinnermaking process.

When my wife cooks a meal she goes really to town. She has mashed potatoes on one burner, broccoli on another, a roast cooking in the oven, then biscuits to follow, and at the same time she's cutting all the veggies to make a salad. The preparation time can take an hour or longer. And then when the kids finish dumping the part that doesn't make it into their mouths onto the floor, you've got another hour to do the cleanup. Of course, don't get me wrong—she loves cooking and does a great job of it, and I really appreciate it. It's just that I don't enjoy cooking as much as she does.

If you don't love cooking, like me, and have ever tried to cook a four-course meal to prove to your wife and to the world that you can do this too, well just stop. The key to making this part of your day easier is to cook one massive meal earlier in the week that will provide you with days of leftovers. For example, make a roast on Monday, then sliced roast on toast on Tuesday. You can eliminate some of the dinner prep and cleanup by making multiple containers of lasagna, chili, spaghetti, or stew dinners and keeping them in the freezer for quick microwave heating. This way you get the convenience of eating out without the costs. To do this, you can make Sunday evening a family cooking evening and all of you can cook a ton of food for the rest of the week—thus creating quality family time, while saving the more valuable weeknight time to just get your daily routines done.

Bedtime Routine

Establishing a bedtime routine is another thing you can do to make both of your lives easier. Kids basically hate to go to bed and will do anything in their power to avoid it. The good news is that kids love routines. Let's say you have kids who will try any excuse to stay awake longer—for example, asking for water breaks, last-minute snacks, or wanting to watch television. If your kids are doing this, then it's time to take the evening schedule into your own hands. In my house the only way to get our sons into bed without them maneu-

Sock Fishing

When my son, Niko (age 3½), started refusing to get out of bed in the morning, I had an idea. Every night I get into bed with my socks on. As I warm up, I kick them off and leave them under the covers and they stay there all night. So when I get up in the morning and go to Niko's room, I say, "Time for sock fishing!" He sprints out of bed to my bed, and we dive under the covers looking for socks. Sometimes they are in the "shallow" end; sometimes way down in the "deep" end. Either way, we crawl around, shouting to each other, until one of us (usually him) finds them and "swims" back up to the surface.

—*Eric Segal, Arlington, Massachusetts*

vering for time is to establish a routine. About an hour before bedtime, we like to have bathtime or at least have them put on their PJs. This gives them fair warning and will slow them down a little. Now they have a whole hour to think about bedtime. Then, about half an hour before bedtime, we have them lie in bed and we read with them. By the time it's lights out, we find that they are pretty calm and they drift off quickly. At first they may complain, but once they get the message that you will not waver in this routine, they will eventually follow the path of least resistance and go with it.

If you are trying to put them to bed an hour or two earlier than their current schedule, ease them into the transition by moving their bedtime back by increments of ten to fifteen minutes each day. Another trick (especially in the summer, when it is sunny out) is to draw the shades so the kids can't see anything that's happening outside. The less distraction, the better. If the television or radio is on in another room when you start your new nighttime routine, turn it off or turn it down so they can't hear it as they start to go to sleep.

My wife and I usually put the kids to bed together. We usually have a short talk with them as they get comfortable in bed. Sometimes I have the best talk of the day with my kids as they grow increasingly tired. After your kids are asleep and it's quiet in the house, this is a good time to talk to your wife and share stories about your day. In our house we sometimes even go to bed shortly after the kids do and talk or read.

When morning comes, you need to reverse the routine. Try to wake them up with a little advance time if they need to go to school. You can do this by just turning on the lights and gently saying it's time to get up. Once they start rolling around, you can play music on a radio or even have the family pet rouse them. Our kids have a pet guinea pig that we will let run under the covers and cuddle. Just don't try to wake your kids up too abruptly. One dad's kid was actually mad at him for waking him up early, so the dad switched to an alarm clock. (When it went off, the dad would say, "It's not my fault that the alarm clock went off, it's the alarm clock's fault!")

A Message for the Moms

Now I want to say a few words to the working moms on helping your husbands and yourselves through this transitional time. There are a number of ways that working moms can alleviate the stress on their at-home husbands. The first thing is to communicate your work schedule and do your best to stick to it. For the at-home dad, simply not knowing when you will be home can throw off the entire night's schedule, such as what time to have dinner prepared. One way to address this is to sit down with your husband every Sunday night and write out a weekly plan. You can post the schedule on the refrigerator and, if changes come up, note them on the posted schedule during the week.

Obviously, things come up and so this will not always work, but at least it will get you both in the habit of making sure you are on the same page. Charles Allen of Dallas, Texas, came up with a good solution.

> I wanted my wife to get home close to when I was expecting her. This way I can plan my life outside of my time alone with my child and I can plan how to pace my kid's energy level during the day. A frustrating situation was resolved when she got her cell phone and I talked her into using it to call me if she was going to be later than expected.

A very simple solution, but it worked!

As important as it is to communicate your work schedule to your husband, you must also relay this message to your boss and coworkers. You may have a demanding job that requires you to stay at the office longer than normal hours. At times there may be emergencies that cannot be avoided. But as the end of your workday approaches, think about what tasks you have in your must-get-done-today pile and which ones you might be able to move into your to-be-done-tomorrow pile. Don't be afraid to tell your boss what expectations you have regarding leaving work for home at the same time each day. Remember, many bosses have families, too, and will sympathize with your cause. Working at a reasonable pace can also be good for your health. The National Institutes for Health released a study in April 2002 that compared women in high-authority jobs with women in low-authority jobs. The women who held high-pressure jobs had three times the risk of heart disease.

In Alexandria, Virginia, Mike Stillwell's wife worked at a frenzied pace as a senior executive at WorldCom, a telecommunications company. She was inundated with high-energy work, phone calls, and e-mails on nights and weekends. When WorldCom went under, she landed a job at Fannie Mae, a company that helps families buy homes, which not only supported her family life, but also encouraged it. Stillwell remarks,

When I left my job to be home with the kids, my wife's realization hit her hard. She was the breadwinner, she had to be careful that she did the best job, so she spent many hours at her work. When she changed jobs to Fannie Mae, they actually urged her to spend more time with the kids. She was able to volunteer for her daughter's soccer team. And to show support, the company donated water and granola bars to the entire team.

(Fannie Mae was named by *Working Mother* magazine in 2002 as one of the top ten best companies for working mothers and was on the top 100 list nine previous times.)

While most moms are not able to control their office cultures, the more balanced your work and family life is, the better and more productive you will feel. Sometimes moms come home in full work mode and continue to act with their children and husbands as they do with their coworkers. For example, one dad complains that his wife, who is a project manager, continues to delegate to him and his children when she gets home. She is still in work mode and needs a cooling off period. He says, "If it means she takes an extra walk around the block before she walks in the door, that's what I wish she would do."

Sometimes working moms who are having trouble adjusting to their new roles outside the home may tell their at-home dads what they could be doing better. To these moms I say: it's time to let go of your old job, especially if you have been the primary caregiver for some time. As you transition back to work, try to avoid supervising your husband. Many husbands feel that their wives don't trust them with their new responsibilities. Gary Foskuhl of Dayton, Ohio, says,

My initial years of staying at home were a constant struggle to live up to my wife's expectations of a parent. Since she could not be at home, she assumed that I would perform in her absence all of the tasks that she felt were essential. I could not do this. I am a different person, a different parent. Eventually, she stopped trying to mold me into her model of a parent. As a result, she began to trust me. She realized that although my parenting style is different, I, too, want the kids to be safe, I also want to educate the kids, and I can also nurture our children. This transformation of trust did not happen overnight. It was a slow and sometimes painful process. In some ways this struggle never stops. But during the third or fourth year, we both came to the conclusion that constant fighting over who was right did little to enhance our family's lifestyle. We finally came to a truce. As a result, we can both focus our efforts on the challenges of raising the children and not the realities of our being different parents.

In his book, *The Man Who Would Be Dad*, Hogan Hilling of Irvine, California writes about his wife Tina's constant reminders to check the kids' diapers, remember naptimes, take extra formula before he goes anywhere, and so forth. Here is his response from his book:

Kid Robots

One day, when my five-year-old son hesitated in eating his broccoli, I told him he was a robot and I would push the right buttons to get the food in his mouth. We both loved it! As I pushed the imaginary buttons on the table and used my thumb as a joystick, I guided the food into his mouth. He actually ate all his broccoli that day.

—*From the Author*

Tina, I understand your concerns about leaving me alone with the boys, but it's a known fact that a baby can survive without food and water for three days. So just go out and have a good time. I promise the boys will still be alive when you get home.

A few weeks later, when they had the same type of discussion, this time about their son's diaper, Hilling recalls,

I explained that . . . it wasn't her unending reminders that finally convinced me to make sure Grant's diaper was on snug enough. It was the mess that I had to clean afterward [if it wasn't]! She explained that she wanted to keep that from happening to me. Of course, I replied. But my feelings are no different from how she feels when her mother gives her advice about how to be a mother. Now Tina understood me. We have to make our own mistakes, with babies as with life.

These constant reminders from working moms can further deflate dads, who often already are dealing with piercing screams from their children crying for their mothers. John Wise of Portland, Maine, describes his frustration:

My three-year-old wants her mom all day. I understand, but it kills me. I have been home for the better part of four years and she still wails for her mom every time she falls or wants something I won't give her. She can't wait for her mom to come home, but it is my name she screams at 3:30 A.M.

As Wise learned, children still turn to their mothers more often for comfort, no matter who the primary caregiver is.

Dr. Robert Frank found in his research that, most of the time, children still turn to their mothers when they wake up at night or go to sleep. To the mothers out there: you may just want to relish these moments, and you should, but you also need to be sensitive to your husbands' feelings. They may already be feeling inadequate and overwhelmed by their new role, and the children's cries for their mother do nothing to make them feel better.

Of course, your husband needs to lovingly reassure you that he now has a better understanding of how challenging a job this is. And, further, he needs to say that he appreciates the job you did before he took over. He needs to let you know how much he appreciates the job you are doing now by taking on the role of breadwinner, which, in turn, makes him feel more comfortable in his role.

Loss of Intimacy

Another source of tension for at-home dads and their working partners is lack of intimacy. While you may have thought that, with the new arrangement, there would be less craziness in your lives, it can still be exhausting for both of you. This on top of the fact that she or both of you may be losing sleep by getting up at night to check on the children or to breastfeed (her, not you), leaves little time for intimacy. At-home dad Joe Finkelstein of Dunwoody, Georgia, says, "Our nine-month-old son, Will, is still breastfeeding. There're usually two long feedings at night and then my wife is pooped. I get resentful sometimes that there's little time and energy on her part for any intimacy."

Ted Pena of Syracuse, New York, offers tips on increasing intimacy:

> We will take day trips in the van just to get an hour or so that we can talk to each other, or even talk over the phone when the timing is right. I imagine that we both believe that as the kids get older this will change a bit. We have found a babysitter so that we can get one or two nights out a month, but that still leaves the everyday time that a couple of any age needs to recharge their relationship.

Bob Jackson of Denver, Colorado, an at-home dad for seven years, says,

> The first eighteen months after having a child, your wife may be so overwhelmed that the only thing she can say no to is sex. Don't worry, intimacy will return, and you will slowly start to reconnect as the kids grow older and demand less attention from you. The circle does come back . . . it's just that when you are in the middle of it, you just can't see it because you are just so friggin' mad.

At times like this it can be hard to keep things in perspective, and by talking it through, you may not be able to change your current situation. Still, at least you will understand each other better, and that can keep the tension down. In the meantime, look for other ways of creating intimacy with your wife. For example, try taking a massage class. Even if she is too tired for intimacy and sex,

Mr. Happy

When my son John was a toddler, he would sometimes get in a foul mood due to hunger or some unknown reason that I couldn't get out of him. I would say, as I pointed at the corner of his mouth, "Hey look! Mr. Happy is trying to get out of your mouth." At this point he is covering his entire face trying not to smile. Then I go in for the kill. "He's getting out! He wants to come out and play on the swings near your ears." By now he's laughing (and eating if he is at the supper table) and suddenly doesn't remember what he was mad about. This worked for me every time.

—*From the Author*

you can at least relax her to sleep and create closeness between the two of you. If setting aside time for a class seems overwhelming, set up some alone time for the two of you. Even if it's just once a month, it can act as something for both of you to look forward to and provide you with some one-on-one time.

Jealous at Home Versus Guilty at Work

There are issues that both you and your working wife will have to work out for yourselves and for your family as a starting point to your new routines. When a father leaves a high-paying, demanding job to take on another with no monetary payment, the chores at home can be very hard to take. But add to that a wife with an equally demanding job, and it can be ego-deflating. Jack Ford of Wilmington, Delaware, who was the head of a crew on a merchant ship, explains how his ego was devastated when he left his job to care for his kids.

> Since the birth of my first child, I had been an active parent, sailing six months and parenting six months a year. The decision to be a twelve-month-a-year parent evolved over time, not at one moment. The most difficult adjustment of full-time parenting was the loss of "status." Having a crew of thirty or forty people who took orders from you was good for ego-building. Having a wife who complains about a stained blouse improperly laundered or children complaining about a meal they didn't like is ego-deflating. I think it is dangerous to take yourself too seriously or have an overinflated ego. Likewise it is a danger to become depressed by lack of self-esteem. Parenting and taking care of a home, cleaning, cooking, laundering are very difficult and very low-status jobs. I sometimes feel I could be replaced and my family better served by a $300-a-week maid.

You may find your role at home a blow to your ego also, but as Ford mentions, you cannot take yourself too seriously.

Mike Stillwell, whom we talked about earlier in this chapter, had the same experiences as Ford. He remembers life before he was an at-home dad. He had two children ages eight and ten and found himself busy working as a fleet manager in charge of maintaining, selling, and purchasing all the city trucks, cars, bulldozers, and "pretty much anything that had wheels on it." His wife was then working at WorldCom and was spending many days traveling cross-country. Due to their busy schedules, their two kids had to go through daycare. "We would both be working and things would always come up such as the kids having a 102° fever, it just never failed." Eight years later, he and his wife had another child. Stillwell says, "I always said that whoever had the lowest wage when the time came would stay home. Summer was coming and the kids were getting out of school, and since I ended up with the lower wage, I came home. Working really wasn't worth it anymore."

At one point, when Stillwell relocated to Texas for his wife's job, it created a rough segment in his life. He reports,

> We had no family, didn't know anybody, and I needed to be with people. Then one week my wife met with her work friends on a three-night management conference in Key West in the middle of the winter! I was resentful and I really hit a low point. It was funny because I would tell my son that sometimes life isn't fair, but after a few days I started saying it to myself out loud. When my wife got home we talked it through, and she let me vent. We realized that what I was doing was best for the family. It doesn't matter if it's not fair, what does matter is that it's best for the family.

You, too, may have to face such realities and accept that life as a stay-at-home dad will not always be perfect.

Just as you thought you'd love your new life role as an at-home dad, most likely your wife was thinking the same thing about rejoining the workforce. Unfortunately, this is rarely the case for mothers at first, since they are dealing with guilt and separation anxiety. While you are dealing with people calling you Mr. Mom and other interesting job titles, your wife has to cope with questions about how good a mother she could possibly be if she is going back to work. Or, for that matter, she might have to live up to coworkers' doubts about her competence in her new job, especially if she has been away from it for some time. Jody Quinn, a working mom from Buffalo, New York, notes,

> The first year was definitely a transition period . . . and not always rosy. Both of us were feeling our ways in our new jobs, each feeling a bit like strangers in a strange land. Interestingly, I think the adjustment was more difficult for me; feeling a little like an interloper returning home to a day of shared experiences, a new way to do Sloppy Joes, and a dishwasher packed in a pattern that only Picasso could create.

Remember to look at your new home life from your wife's perspective.

Often, working mothers experience intense jealousy issues, wishing that they were the ones at home with the kids. Just as you might feel resentful of her for getting out of the house, your wife may feel some resentment toward you for getting to be with the children all day long. One dad sums it up this way: "My wife is insanely jealous that I am at home with the kids, and I'm jealous that she gets to go to work every day." In some cases moms may be jealous that you are spending time at the playground with other moms as well as dads. To relieve her of her fears, take her to the playground and have her meet the other moms. Maybe she can help you get in with some of the women. Seeing you with your wife might soften them up.

To help your wife feel that she is not being ripped apart from her children, you may need to work extra hard to make her feel like she is part of the family. Here are a few suggestions to let Mom know she is still loved:

- Have the kids do projects for Mom, such as write "Welcome Home" cards and signs or draw pictures for her. This achieves two purposes: it will keep the children occupied and quiet for a few hours, and it will make your wife feel good.
- Schedule mommy time. Again, another suggestion with a dual purpose. By allotting a day, morning, or evening each week for your wife to spend with the kids, you not only are giving her the quality time she wants with the children, but you are also giving yourself a break.
- Make sure to involve your wife in your daily child-rearing decisions. Even though you are the parent home with the kids all day, make an effort to include your wife in every decision. Parenting, no matter who spends more time with the children, is a team effort, and she will feel better knowing that you still rely on her judgment.
- Send e-mails to your wife if she is working late. If your wife uses e-mail, send your wife a picture of the kids showing what they were doing that day. Take a photograph of your kids holding their school art projects and fire off that .jpg file to her. It will create a nice moment for your wife at work, and she will thank you when she gets home . . . even if she does get home late.
- Schedule a date night. It doesn't have to be front row seats at a Rolling Stones concert (but that would be OK, too). A date can be an opportunity for you to talk in a dining area that doesn't have applesauce on the floor.

There are going to be times when you and your wife both just want to vent—she about how messy you are, and how she misses the kids, and so on, and you about how you are feeling isolated, are sick of the kids, and feel underappreciated. Many dads find that counseling can be a huge help in getting a lot off their chests. Sometimes going to your wife with all of your frustrations and anger may not be the best solution. Being able to go and talk to an objective third party can help you keep things in perspective. Seeing a therapist can also be a valuable resource for your wife if she is having a hard time adjusting to her new role. Whether it's something the two of you do together or apart, it is a great way to keep your perspective during a time that can often be harrowing.

While the jealousy and the adjustments might be putting your marriage in turmoil, do not forget that the kids are the reason you

Sleepy Dolls

Recently I've had trouble putting Jena, my twenty-one-month-old daughter, to bed at night. All the experts say, "Establish a routine for bedtime." Well, my wife and I tried reading her a story and saying a prayer. Then she'd send up a wail of woe and cry as if her heart were broken as soon as we left the room. The other night I collected her favorite dolls and stuffed animals and brought them to her crib. I tucked them all in, told them it was time to go "night night," shushed them, and said "Aw, good babies." Jena loved this and repeated what I had told them. I picked her up and snuggled her in between her little friends. I said, "Night night," shushed her, and told her what a good baby she was. I left the room expecting to hear the usual lament at any moment. I didn't. She went right to sleep. This "routine" has worked now for four nights in a row.

—Daniel B. Chapman, South Bend, Indiana

are doing all of this, and that they most likely will be the most affected by the role reversal. The best thing that parents can do is be open with them and try not to hide the fact that this is difficult for the two of you. At-home dad Mark Abraham of Minneapolis, Minnesota, dealt with this issue by instructing his 4½-year-old son, "if Mommy or Daddy start using a mean voice, let us know." One time, after he told his son this, he and his wife were arguing at the dinner table and his son suddenly called out, "Mommy! Daddy! Remember friendly voices!" A few ground rules that Abraham suggests to keep your disagreements with each other separate from your role as parents are:

- Keep your disagreements out of the sound range of kids.
- Do not intervene right there if you think your wife is "solving a kid problem incorrectly." Talk about it later to set up new ground rules.
- When you do talk, keep your communication open, honest, and consistent, since your expectations will change over time.
- Also, admit to your wife when you are wrong. Yes, I know this is a toughie, but it will save you hours, if not days, of grief.

Communication is key to sustaining this new family structure, and being able to speak your concerns, feel like you're being heard, and not feel like you are being judged are all important elements in making this new formula work.

Discipline

As part of your game plan to help your kids adjust to your new roles, you also need to work together to discuss how you will discipline your children. Using the contract in this chapter can help you share the discipline duties. It will help you and your wife communicate when you need to discipline the kids. If you previously left all the disciplinary actions to your wife, this may be the biggest challenge for you. Being consistent with your warnings and punishments is essential, no matter how angry or frustrated you get. Keeping your cool will be hard, but it's important to be effective. If you lose your patience too quickly, it can result in screaming fights, temper tantrums, and overall a lot of behaviors you would rather avoid. Here are some survival tips from dads. These are recommendations you can use before you lose your patience:

- Take a deep breath and leave the room when you feel the impulse to react and raise your voice. Then get down to eye level with your child, put your hand on his/her shoulder, and whisper to him/her.
- If the kids are fighting, split them up and count to ten while you decompress.
- Call a "time out" for yourself and ask your wife to cover for you for a few minutes.
- Make sure the kids are not hungry for a midday snack.
- Turn on the silly switch in your head. Turn off being an adult and turn on a kid button (easier said than done). In other words, think like a kid. Remember they love to have fun, and have fun with them.

Jay Westra of Carol Stream, Illinois, recognizes his impatience when he is attempting to clean or fix an item. "My daughter will be in my face attempting 'to help' but will create a larger mess. My solutions? I think calm thoughts and try to be patient and understanding—take a breath, and later talk about the moment (not during the moment). Discussion seems to work." By calmly talking to his daughter, Westra is able to help his child understand what made him feel impatient and helps her avoid the same situation the next time.

Back to Bed!

When our son developed an ear infection, he began midnight trips to us looking for comfort. We welcomed him to our bed since we enjoyed cozying up. When he got better, he continued this routine, which caused us all to lose sleep. When we returned him to his crib, he screamed hysterically, hopped out, and climbed back in bed with us. What to do?

Our solution: every time he went to our bed, we quietly and gently picked him up and returned him to bed. After fifteen return trips with a gentle reminder that he must sleep in his crib, he finally tired out, fell asleep, and has been fine since. Although he got the message in one night, we got a real lesson in patience.

—From the Author

Teamwork, and a lot of patience, will help you and your wife through this life change. Joel Axler of Rosemont, Pennsylvania, says that by working closely with his wife, he believes that in the end, his family and marriage have grown even stronger.

Our situation, with me at home, takes a greater amount of communication and patience with one another. In our family, there was no model for this level of involvement of the father. Consequently, problems occur as my wife and I share in the responsibility of raising our child. We have to collaborate more and solve problems that develop from our different perspectives. Though at times these difficulties occur, I believe there is no greater, more honorable task than raising a child. And it doesn't hurt that our son, Joshua, is so damn cute!

I hope this chapter helped you lighten up a little if you are stressed out in your new role as an at-home dad. In the next chapter I will examine the sensitive subject of housecleaning.

SPOTLIGHT ON DAD

"Beer in the Fridge/Breast Milk in the Freezer"

By David Bulley   *David Bulley of Montague, Massachusetts, is an at-home dad to two boys. He's a freelance writer, publishing mostly short fiction. You can read a sample chapter of his latest novel,* Weapon in Heaven, *at www.davidbulley.com or contact him at Dave@Bulleys.com.*

This memory haunts and comforts me: I am pacing the floor holding my three-month-old son. He is hungry. I know he is hungry. I have been home with him since his birth, and the signs are clear. Frozen breast milk is in the freezer, but each small baggy is more precious than gold and my wife will be home in five minutes. He is crying. My wife has been working, as much as she can, around a quickly imposed breastfeeding schedule. My son adapted well, but this is cutting it close and he is hungry. I pace the floor holding his crumpled, crying body against my chest and trying to comfort him, but he is not crying for comfort. He's crying for food.

She is five minutes late now, and my son feeds off my anxiety as well as his hunger, and cries all the louder. Maybe I should have fed him. But she will surely be home soon and I would hate to give him a bottle one second before she walks in the door. He grows more distraught, so I hold his tiny head against my chest to protect his fragile neck and leap straight into the air. I land hard and he stops crying. He begins crying again and my pacing quickens. I bounce up and down as I walk. I sing through my panting. I rock side to side. I cannot comfort him because he is hungry and my wife is now fifteen minutes late and I should have fed him. Each minute that I put him off is one more minute until she will be home, so I am trapped in this terrible cycle of depriving my son.

I hold my son in my left arm and, as I pass from the kitchen into the living room for the thousandth time, I punch the wall hard enough to break the Sheetrock, hurt my fist, and startle my son. He cries louder. She is a half-hour late. I lean my head against the cold of the window and watch for her car. I have given up trying to console my son. When my wife finally bursts through the door and removes her coat, I see that milk has completely soaked through her shirt. I have no pity. She is trying to tell me what happened, but I thrust my crying son into her arms and run out the door. From the day my first son was born I vowed never to let him see me smoke, and when my hands stop shaking enough, I light my first cigarette of the day.

When I go back into the house, my son is sleeping. That was the day I stopped being a glorified babysitter and became the primary caregiver of my child. From that day forward, with my first and then with my second son, when they were hungry, I fed them. When the doctor said it was OK, I began to supplement breast milk with formula so that I would never have to worry about having enough. If they were hungry two minutes before my wife was due home, I fixed them a bottle and let her pump. I will never forget how I felt as soon as I made that decision. I was no longer just responsible for my child's safety when my wife was working. I was responsible for his care.

My father's job was to earn money. Sometimes, if my mother had to go out, my father made sure my brothers and I were safe until her return. He was a babysitter. I remember him wrinkling his nose and handing off my youngest brother to have his diaper changed. I wonder if he felt frustrated and powerless. I wonder if he went to work and pounded machinery, venting rage at feelings of inadequacy. I hope he did not. When I first became a father, there were so many things I thought that a man could not or should not do for his children. I was amazed that my hands could be gentle enough to bathe an infant. I thought that there was some unwritten rule that men must gag if they were forced into changing a diaper. I held an irrational belief that women possessed some secret knowledge of comforting crying children. In some ways, our society keeps trying to give these beliefs back to me.

My children are now six and four years old, and it is still mildly frustrating when a kindly older woman in the grocery store asks if I am babysitting today, or when a strange woman volunteers to hold my crying child in the playground after he has fallen and hurt himself. When my wife and I take our children to the doctor, he or she always asks my wife what the symptoms are and when their last bowel movements were. My wife looks at me and I give the answer. The doctor asks the next question, still looking at my wife for the answer.

Sometimes I speak up. More often, I just let it pass. I am not sure when, if ever, things will be any different, but I know this: now and forever, when my children are hungry, I will feed them.

3

Men Who Clean Bathrooms and the Women Who Love Them

My first lesson in cleaning bathrooms occurred long before I was married. I was working at a Denny's restaurant as a busboy, trying to earn money for college. I was by far the low man on the totem pole there, and this was made clear by the tasks I was given. My primary responsibility was to bring the dirty dishes to the dishwasher. That was a thrill a minute compared to my other job, which was to clean the bathrooms. The manager who was training me brought me to the ladies room, where he showed me how to use a toilet brush and scrub the bowls clean. When he was done, he said that the most important thing about my job was to make sure the ladies' bathroom was always clean, because this was the number one complaint that came from female customers. "Don't worry about the men's room," he said. "The men never complain."

About fifteen years, a wedding, and one baby later, my wife started pressing me to clean the bathrooms. I had just gotten a handle on washing the dishes and was still struggling with making dinner—but cleaning the bathrooms? Even though I practically had a degree in toilet cleaning, I cringed at the idea and put it off as long as possible. That was when I realized how much lower my cleaning standards were compared to those of my wife. I could relate to humorist Dave Barry, when he said that he wouldn't notice that the kitchen floor was dirty until there was a garden growing in the dirt. "Aha," I thought. "I can just wait for her to do it." That plan backfired after a few weeks, however, as I realized that every time she found herself cleaning something, she would get more and more frustrated, and eventually we would have an argument.

I realized that if my wife noticed clutter when she first walked into the house, she would assume that the whole house was messy (which it was). So I decided to clean the first thing she saw when she entered, to give her a moment of peace—before the utter chaos of the house was revealed. This meant all I had to clean was the kitchen table and the shelves on the wall behind it. I would quickly distract her with kisses and hugs, and that would set the tone for the evening. One day my timing was off, and before I had a chance to do my cleaning I saw her walking up the driveway. The kitchen was a mess! I scanned the room for something to save me—when my eyes caught our pair of candlesticks. I grabbed them and lit them and put them on the kitchen table. Then I turned the radio on and tuned in a jazz station. Last (and this is crucial), I shut the lights off. Not only had I created a nice, romantic atmosphere for her to come home to, but also she wouldn't be able to see the mess that was our house through the soft glow of the candles! Since she would be tired after a long day of work, I suggested she go upstairs and relax while I prepare supper. This was very effective, since it gave me the extra time to finish cleaning up. Of course, you can't whip up such subterfuge for an indefinite period of time. I realized that in the long run it was important to keep the house clean—for the sake of our marriage, if nothing else.

For many of us, cleaning the house requires a whole new education. We grew up with traditional gender roles, according to which we would play with our plastic lawnmowers while the girls would pretend to cook in the kitchen. Jim Mains of Oak Park, Illinois, agrees, "Most boys didn't clean. Boys were out cutting the grass, emptying the garbage, and such, while most girls were given the domestic chores of cleaning and cooking." So it's no wonder that we might feel we are going against the grain of male expectations now that it's our turn to do the cleaning.

In this chapter I will explore other dads' definitions of "clean" and show how you can adjust to your wife's standards of cleaning. I will look at childproofing, setting a schedule, the wife's point of view, and even hiring a housecleaner. This should help you work together to make things cleaner and clutter-free.

Living Up to a Higher Standard of Cleaning

As I mentioned in Chapter 2, I have gone through periods when my wife gave me "the talk" about my poor cleaning habits. But since I had no one else with whom to compare myself, I never really knew if my standard of cleaning was set too low or if my wife's was set too high. I needed reassurance—something, anything—that would help me feel better about my cleaning habits. So as I've done for so many other issues, I put the question to the readers of the *At-Home Dad Newsletter* to hear what my comrades had to say.

Bottom Drawer Blues

Are you tired of keeping your toddler out of your bottom drawer in the kitchen? Don't fight it, just take whatever you deem harmless (like Tupperware, plastic bottles, wooden spoons, empty diaper wipe containers, and so forth) and fill up the drawer. The next time your kid opens the drawer, you don't have to say "*No!*" Just sit back and enjoy the show.

—From the Author

After I checked with at-home dads across the country, I found they were almost unanimous in stating that their wives' cleaning habits were too high. Here are some of the replies I received:

- Jon Harper of Milwaukee, Wisconsin, whose wife used to be a professional housecleaner, writes: "My wife seems to see things that no one else can see, and she looks at any space in a different way. I just miss a lot, mostly because I clean what I can see. She cleans around, behind, and above everything. I clean the floors and low things that I look at. She starts at the ceiling and cleans down."
- Another dad, Kevin Kush of Indianapolis, Indiana, says the main problem is clutter. "I make sure the house is clean of dirt and grime, but it is the clutter that she [his wife] has had a hard time dealing with. By clutter, I mean toys and ongoing building and science projects. Naptime is the time I pick up the clutter. I make sure that I keep all the clothes clean and put away, and that dinner is ready when she gets home."
- "I wouldn't say my wife has a higher standard of house-cleaning," says Jim Mains. "Just a difference in opinion on the definition of the word *clean*."

Some dads find that the definition of the word *clean* can vary wildly depending upon the area of the house. "My wife tolerates clutter far better than I," says Dan Dunsmore of Charlottesville, Virginia. "But she absolutely cannot tolerate soiled kitchen sinks, stoves, bathroom sinks, showers, or toilets. When the cleaning of the house is left to me, we are lucky to find even one magazine lying on any table, but we constantly find a greenish mold creeping out of the toilet. When my wife cleans, we cannot even find the tables because of all of the old newspapers, magazines, shoes, plates, and coffee cups, but we could probably safely eat out of our bathroom sinks."

I have found from the dads above and many others I have talked to that housecleaning is a hot-button topic in many at-home dad households. With a role reversal, this is bound to happen and is one of the major sources of arguments and frustration.

The Wife's Point of View

When you have put in a full day of childcare work, it can be hard to hear any complaints from your wife. One dad notes his wife's major complaint is that she does not get enough help. Also, he says, "There are things that she feels she should not have to ask to have done or help with. Example: one of my oldest son's jobs is to take out the trash. He has to be told every day to look at the trash and take it out. That can lead to other things that never get done that are obvious." On the other side of the spectrum, Jason Kauflin of Milwaukee, Wisconsin, says, "My wife's major complaint is that I have too many systems for keeping the house in order. She thinks I am borderline obsessive-compulsive. I will make a comment if she puts the paper towels or toilet paper on backward."

If you are both basically doing your jobs—that is, if she continues to bring home the paycheck and helps out a little bit around the house, and you continue to give your kids good, quality care and attention and do your best to pick up and clean with the energy you have left over—you may still get complaints from your partner. Because everyone has a different system to get things done, a unique timetable, and different standards, it's unlikely that you and your partner will always see eye-to-eye when it comes to cleaning. Learning to accept each other's standard of cleanliness and trying to look at the situation objectively will help you survive the most challenging years, when your children require the most time and attention—and when they make the most mess. But if one of you suddenly alters how much you do in the cleaning or paycheck-earning department, then it's time to have an honest discussion and possibly reevaluate the chores that each of you takes on. Remember to pay attention to your wife's point of view. She works hard, too, and even thirty minutes to an hour of cleaning toward the end of the day will give her the clean environment she deserves.

Resolving Your Differences

Some dads have found that the best way to learn how to clean is to ask for feedback on ways to improve the job they're doing. When Casey Spencer of Los Angeles asked if his wife objected to any of his cleaning habits, she responded with a list of her complaints: "A: Laundry; left incomplete and cluttering the house. B: Dishes; left incomplete and cluttering the kitchen. C: Picking up the house; not done in time for company. A biggie. D: Laundry; damaged/stained her or baby's clothing." Here's an example of how to address one of these complaints—for good. The laundry complaint could be eliminated if his wife tagged her clothing items with "pre-spot" or "minor inconsequential stain under left armpit," just as the drycleaner expects us to point such things out. Or you may feel bold and confident enough to ask for a miniseminar on laundry so that you can learn what to look for—and then do it!—instead of asking for guidance each time. It may not be the most pleasant conversation you have with your wife, but at least it can provide you with a foundation from which to build.

Toilet Target Practice

Here's one dad's solution to the poor-aim toilet problem. "My seven-year-old son urinates everywhere but in the toilet. I drape toilet paper over the seat and with a marker I draw a simple circle with a dot in the middle. It's big enough for my son to have success aiming, and the supply of targets is always at your fingertips. He giggled the first time we tried it."

—*Mark Baron, Sharon, Massachusetts*

And as long as you realize you both play on the same team—you both want clean clothes and a happy home—you can work together to make things better.

Often your wife will have to adjust to your cleaning habits. Perhaps you put the laundry in different drawers than she would have, or the bed is made differently. These are things that she may just have to live with now that you are the home keeper. Jim Mains says that the only thing that came close to an argument with his wife was over how to fold the towels. "Basically we settled the issue when it was determined that I did the laundry and thus I determine how it is folded." Dan Dunsmore fares even better, saying his wife wouldn't dare lodge any complaints. "I don't tell her how [to do her job], and she better not say a word about the mold."

Getting the Kids to Help

A great way to keep the kids from messing up the house is to have them actually clean the house. Of course, this applies to kids who are old enough to help out, and you'll need to use your own judgment, depending on the maturity of your child. But even simple chores can be mastered by three- and four-year-olds. For example, one dad makes it a game with his toddler, who is now learning to fold laundry and is already putting toys away. Bob Lang of Aberdeen, Maryland, says, "By making a game out of chores, sticking to one task at a time, and supplementing cleanup with gobs of praise, I encourage my three-year-old to help with basic tasks. My idea was to fashion a hoop over a toy box and score points on a chalkboard for toys properly placed, or an even more elaborate set-up is to use a large piece of cardboard or wood with a funny monster painted on the surface. Use the mouth as the hole. How many toys can the toy monster eat?" One dad even had a two-year-old "telling Mom to put something away."

Another overwhelming favorite I've heard from dads is to use the vacuuming power of pets to clean the floor. "You need a dog to keep the discarded Cheerios eaten," says one dad. Of course, be careful of overusing this method—the last thing you want is to have your dog puke all over your nice, clean kitchen floor!

My two boys love to dump their jackets and backpacks onto our breezeway floor when they come home from school. After telling them for a week to hang up their coats, they would still absent-mindedly throw them on the floor. One day, I waited for the coats to hit the floor and I activated the "coat alarm," which was my best imitation of an annoyingly bad car alarm. By making it a funny game, they remember the annoying coat alarm will be screaming in their ears and they end up hanging up their coats. My boys will test it now and then by intentionally dropping their coats on the floor, and now we all end up in fits of giggles. We have expanded this concept to improve their eating habits. Every time they eat with their fingers, the "finger alarm" is triggered. Kids love games of all kinds, so if you can create one to help clean the house

---

Animal Showers

I had to figure out a way to take a shower while I was taking care of Niko (four years old), and I finally came up with something that works. When I'm ready to shower, I ask him if he will come in to help me. When I get in, I cry out, "It's too hot!" and he tells me to turn up the cold. Then it's too cold, and so on. Well, this is fun, but it gets old quickly. So then I say, "There're mosquitoes coming out!" and he says, "Better turn on the bats to eat them!" Then, "There're mice coming out!" and he says, "Better turn on the cats to get them!" We go through all kinds of animals, and what they get eaten by. So not only do I get to take a shower, but also Niko learns about the food chain! Latest: "There're too many apatosauruses in here!" "Better turn on the T. rexes!"

—*Eric Segal, Arlington, Massachusetts*

(or to keep it clean) while giving them a little fun in the process, that seems to be the best plan of all.

For some dads, it's easier to do one big cleanup once a week than to constantly clean up all week. One father I spoke to put together a "cleaning mix"—a medley of his favorite songs that he can play while he cleans the house. When done right, cleaning can be highly cathartic!

Another dad makes cleaning a race with his kids. Every room is assigned to a child and one to himself and they race to clean—whoever cleans his or her room the fastest (with the approval of the rest of the competitors that the room is actually clean) wins. Another idea is to play army platoon, in which you are the drill sergeant and call out "inspection," and your kids then have an hour to clean their rooms. When time is up, you come in and inspect what kind of job each child did. This can become an ongoing game in which your kids can accrue points and win prizes of your choosing.

Any way that you make cleaning fun—whether thinking about your own needs or those of your kids—will make you a happier man. And making cleaning fun will make it more of a joy than a chore. Don't surrender to the gods of drudgery—you're sacrificing precious hours out of your day that you'll never get back. So fight back by making it fun!

Childproofing

A good preventive measure to help you avoid cleaning is childproofing the house. Victor Bennett of Camden, New Jersey, a father of four grown children, ages twenty-five to thirty-three, and now a fourteen-month-old, has learned from experience. His solutions?

- If a child should not have an item, then it goes out of reach. Use the locked or childproof kitchen cabinet fixtures if necessary.
- If you find yourself saying "no" (certainly if it's "NO!"), save the "no" and put the thing somewhere

else. This way your child can have the freedom to roam in your childproof rooms without too many restricting gates or closed doors, and without coming to think that "no" is a big person's primary form of communication.

- By setting up rooms, play areas, trips, events, and more, the little ones we love so much can do what *they* need to do: be curious, explore, learn, grow, feel they're a part of what's around them, and feel safe and loved.

These are just a few ideas. Remember to use the other dads in your playgroup or find dads online for more ideas.

Setting a Schedule

I've found that the best way for me to organize my day is to make a list of things I want to accomplish that day. In the morning I will write down all of the tasks I need to do around the house and add them to a list of appointments or other commitments outside the house. My wife adds in additional things she wants me to do. I make each item on my list a manageable size. For example, I'd never write down "clean the house" because it would take me forever to do this and it would be unlikely that I could get it done. So I break down my list of tasks to manageable-sized chores, such as "dry mop the kitchen floor" instead of "dust and mop the floors." This also gives me the great pleasure of crossing items off the list as I complete each task. This sense of accomplishment helps when there is a mountain of laundry, piles of toys, and the kitchen looks like an explosion went off last week and the residue has become crusty and hardened. Making a list helps me remember things, too, in case I get distracted.

Here are tips from other dads regarding scheduling:

- Several dads suggested making a schedule and sticking to it, but also being prepared to spot-clean, too. Just do what it says for the given day and forget about the rest.

- When you see something's dirty, clean it. Even if it's not on your schedule. Even if you'd rather not. Do it.
- Use a calendar program on the computer to do the scheduling.
- Load up on the videos and do the major cleaning in one day.

Cleaning Tips from Other Dads

Here are more cleaning tips from other at-home dads.

From Jon Harper of Milwaukee, Wisconsin:

- Start at the top, clean down, and then vacuum the floors.
- Look for problem areas and find a way to solve the problem. Example: Our bathroom mirror always had white toothpaste spots on it. My solution was to have the kids spit into the bathtub. It was much easier to rinse out the tub than to clean the mirror.
- Another one was my irritation with all the toys in the yard. I bought two large trashcans and drilled holes in the bottom to let out the rainwater. I had the kids put all the yard toys away in the trashcans, which would include toys belonging to all the kids in the neighborhood. At times some parents come over and look for their kids' missing toys in our "toy bins."

From Jason Kauflin:

- I recommend buying a plastic tub with a handle to carry all of your cleaning supplies in; it helps keep you organized.
- On days when you are not doing any major cleaning, I would also suggest that dads try to spend five to ten

minutes cleaning and straightening right before Mom gets home from work. You know things aren't clean, but when Mom walks in and sees things in order she thinks you have been working hard all day.

- I make a point to make the bed and have all clothes off the floor and put away in the bedroom. I think when she gets home from work and goes in to change, it subconsciously relaxes her.

Toilet habits are a particularly touchy topic for most wives. During an online chat about housecleaning, one dad claimed that his five-year-old son "has bad aim." Then a mom chimed in that her husband has the same problem. She wrote, "What kills me is he lifts the seat to pee and *sees* that nasty bottom, but won't clean it!!!" I then asked her, "If you never cleaned it till it really stunk, would he clean it?" She responded, "I doubt it could ever get stinky enough for a man who claims he can't smell a poopy diaper!" She insisted, "He would ignore it at any rate . . . even if he couldn't stand the smell!" So dads, if you cannot manage to get to any other cleaning, then at a minimum, please make sure your wife comes home to a toilet that is clean!

And of course don't rule out getting a housecleaner. Andy Ferguson of Kansas City, Missouri, says,

Whatever your indulgence is, do a little bit less of it and put the money toward a cleaning person to come in a few times a month for a few hours and at least do the heavy cleaning. It makes it much easier to keep up with the light cleaning and takes enormous pressure off everybody. Don't bother with the commercial/franchise services; they charge an obscene hourly rate, and for what you pay them you could have a private individual come for three to four times the hours. If you can't find the money in the budget, just remember next time you order out for pizza that you just paid yourself for scrubbing the toi-

---

Creative Trash

The first art scribbling my son made ended up in the main gallery, in the kitchen, under a banana magnet on the refrigerator. As he grew older, the artwork became more sophisticated—for example, the seven toilet paper tubes he taped together (a spaceship) or the wet toilet paper held together by an entire roll of Scotch tape (a boat). Soon I was overwhelmed and had to reluctantly start throwing them away, since I had absolutely no place left on my wall or shelf to display them. Trouble is, I never knew when he would remember something he made, so I started a box or a holding area where I would store his works of art for two weeks. If he doesn't mention it in two or three weeks, then it's out the door.

—From the Author

---

lets (and you don't get to order two just because your toddler is potty training).

Getting your kids to help when possible, and putting yourself in your wife's shoes will help you create a satisfying balance in the cleanliness of your home environment.

Just as this chapter ends with the voices of other dads and their tips, take heed. Be man enough to learn from others. Your fellow at-home dads are a good source of advice. Your library has books on home repair and cleaning, too. Call your mother—she would love to help you. I bet your father would, too. And even closer still is the Internet, for the next time you need advice on a nontoxic solution to unclogging your drain when your wife is due home within the hour.

Cleanliness is important, but it's not instinctual. It's a learned behavior. And just as you've learned to live with your wife and learned to adjust your home life to make room for your children, so, too, can you make room for cleaning. That way everyone else will have a little more room to enjoy family time. I hope this chapter has helped get you on your way. In the next chapter I will show you how to start new connections and even join or start up your own playgroup.

SPOTLIGHT ON DAD
"Why Is It?"

BY JOHN WISE   *John Wise has been home with his son, Jack, and daughter, Ellen Grace, since June of 1994. He now runs his wife's business, Medical Staffing Services of Maine, out of his Brunswick, Maine, home.*

Why is it that I can never find *anything*? I mean, I *am* the one who is at home. I should know where things are. Instead, when my wife, Julie, decides to do a "deep cleaning" (as opposed to my surface cleaning), she moves all the stuff and tells me that *she* can reach or find it easier. I then must state the obvious: "Julie, when was the last time you actually used _____ (insert any kitchen utensil, floor cleaner, mop, dish detergent, laundry detergent, book, TV switcher, CD, or potholder)?"

Why is it that what is dear always gets broken? It's never a toy. They're all made of indestructible plastic these days. My prize possession is a framed photo of Bobby Orr flying through the air as he scores the Stanley Cup overtime winning goal against the St. Louis Blues in 1970. It is not so much the fact that the glass broke after my son knocked it off the wall that made me angry. He felt as bad as I. I was upset that $15 turned to $70. I went to the frame shop. The very nice people there quoted me $15 for new glass. Of course there was a bubble in the photo, and the mat board was eating away at the edges (at least that's what he said, I could not see it). Well, new glass, untreated mat board, borders, and $70 later, I walked from the frame shop feeling a bit naked. Needless to say, Julie does all the big-ticket purchasing in this house.

Why is it that my kids want to help when it is the least helpful? This is especially true when I am trying to put together toys that come in seventy-five pieces. I suppose I should welcome and honor the help. I do sometimes. Occasionally though, my red level peaks soon after Ellen Grace has removed all the stickers that were to be placed carefully on her vanity and stuck them on the kitchen floor. Cleaning tip: If you are not picky about the appearance of your kitchen floor, don't try to pry these gems up. If you are, get 'em up quick. The adhesive on this stuff is truly amazing.

4

Making New Connections

Like many other at-home dads, I felt isolated when I began this new career. Indeed, isolation is the number one complaint among at-home dads during their first year, as we saw in Chapter 1. While at my former office job, it was easy to network with others. We were all in the same building, we all had similar gripes about our days, and there was that common bond that comes with working together in an office—meetings, lunchtime, and parties brought us together. When I started out at home, I longed for that kind of adult conversation. One night I even dreamt I was back at work enjoying conversation with my coworkers.

In this chapter I will talk about the various ways dads can make new connections with others now that they are at home. I will show you your options, ranging from joining or starting a playgroup to having a night out with other dads to even learning to hang out with the moms at the playgrounds. I will also show you how dads are able to connect using Internet message boards.

Playgroups

A 2002 study issued by the National Institutes for Health shows that at-home dads have an 82 percent increase in the risk of developing coronary artery disease due to "increased levels of stress." The research cites that a way to lower this stress is to participate in a dad's playgroup, which will in essence provide some type of outlet and support system for dads.

One at-home dad playgroup in Atlanta was interviewed by CNN for a story, and the dads discussed how participating in the group has helped them adjust to their new roles. "Keeps my sanity," said one dad. Peter Steinberg of Springfield, Virginia, founder of the D.C. Metro Dads Playgroup in the Washington, D.C., area, said,

> Playgroups help me stay away from the feelings of isolation and stress. I enjoy talking to other adults more than anything else. It's also important for kids to see other kids, too. It got me out of the house. If I knew I was getting out of the house, it just gave me a goal to look forward to.

You, too, might find that joining a playgroup helps you maintain your sanity.

I discovered these playgroups during my first year in my new role, back in 1995. By luck, I came across an article in the *Boston Globe* featuring an at-home dads' playgroup run by Peter Allen of North Reading, Massachusetts. Frustrated with some of the mothers' groups he attended, he began using his home as a meeting place, and he had been at it for five years when I first saw him. When I brought my two-year-old son, John, for our first visit, I felt like I was going to my first day on the job. Having no idea of what to expect or what kind of men I was about to encounter, I took the plunge. Upon walking in, John eagerly ran off to the spacious living room to play with Allen's five-year-old twin sons, Zachary and Matthew. It was such a relief to let him go and not have to run after him. I chatted with Allen and another dad who had been dropping by for the last four years with his son and daughter. My initial anxiety went away quickly in meeting the dads, as we got into a discussion comparing our wives' cleaning habits. Allen, who teaches piano part-time "for his sanity," has been staying home with his sons since they were born. He states, "The group is just that, a group, no meeting plans or formal structure. Just enter and talk." He has had from one to five dads show up on a given day. Some have since gotten jobs or moved away.

Soon after I joined the group, another dad found out about us and came aboard with his eight-month-old daughter in tow. "The benefit is great," he says of the playgroup. "I've noticed my daughter is more alert now as she watches and plays with others. I enjoy getting out of the house and making new friendships."

Starting Your Own Playgroup

Organizing men is hard. Organizing at-home dads is even harder. Two million years ago, when we were hunter-gatherer dads, we wouldn't ask for help because that would signal vulnerability—especially in unknown terrain where the inhabitants might be unfriendly and show this by, say, eating you. This survivalist trait stopped being necessary a few thousand years ago, but it may take a few thousand more years to wipe this trait out of our male genes. (This means that in a few hundred years we may be driving to the wrong planet in our spacecraft, even after our wives have already told us five times that we already passed Jupiter.) With this reluc-

Bookwork

A great way to meet others is to volunteer one morning a week at the library reshelving DVDs and VHS tapes. I bring my son with me—he loves it, and he can meet other kids as well.

—*Keith Poole, Chicago, Illinois*

tance to ask for directions comes an inability to reach out for support in the way women can and do.

However, reaching out is the first step to sanity for many at-home dads. If you don't have luck finding a group as I did, or feel out of place in a mothers' group, you need to take the offensive and start your own. (See the resource listing in the back of the book for information on how to find existing playgroups in your area.) Basically, the hardest part is getting over your own inability to reach out for support. After you do that, it's really just a matter of taking advantage of the resources around you. Here are some suggestions on how to get a playgroup up and running:

- Advertise. Put up a flyer in your town library, in its children's room or play area. You can also place an ad in your local newspaper. They will probably offer you this service for free if you explain your situation personally. The ad can look something like this: "Looking to form an at-home dad playgroup for fathers who are primary caregivers for their children. This weekly playgroup will provide fun and support for you and your children. Please call John Doe at 555-1212 for more information."
- Check with local mothers' resource groups that may meet in your local church, library, or school. They may know a few at-home dads who are also looking to connect.
- Contact local hospitals. Why not start where it all begins? While most hospitals have a ton of support groups for moms, many do not have similar programs for dads, let alone at-home dads. Talk to the counselors at the hospital about starting such a group, and then work to publicize it in the local papers. No one will be more willing to join a group for at-home dads than one who is expecting.

- Tell others you meet during your regular trips to the playground (especially any men you meet with kids in tow) about your group. Word of mouth travels fast.
- Look online. There are hundreds of resources for at-home parents on the Web. Check out the At-Home Dad Network at www.athomedad.com to see if there is a playgroup in your area.

One of the most effective ways to start or expand your playgroup is to use the media. Casey Spencer and Jim DiCenzo cofounded a playgroup chapter in San Diego and started a second chapter in Los Angeles with the help of the media. When Spencer was trying to get media coverage, he would pay attention to the articles written in the local papers and to who the reporters were. He says,

In Los Angeles, I wrote a response to an *L.A. Times* Careers section article, which asked readers, "How do you keep family/career balance in your home?" The *Times* called, sent a photographer, and ran a few paragraphs. This generated nearly a dozen contacts and added several guys to my group. Just by writing to the "local activities" columnist for our local Glendale (California) area, I got a mention as well.

Getting the media interested in your choice to be an at-home dad is one way to garner more attention for the choice in general and, more specifically, this may provide you with the opportunity to get the word out about your group.

The First Meetings

OK, so you placed the ads, made a successful pitch to the media, got a few calls—now where to begin? What to do? Mike Stillwell of Alexandria, Virginia, recommends that for the first few meet-

---

Sea School

If you visit the ocean, here's a way to test your kids' math skills. Go close to where the tide is moving in and out, wait for a wave to go out, and write a math problem in the sand with your finger such as "4+4=." Now tell your children to write the answer in the sand with their fingers before the next wave comes in and washes the numbers away. This challenge will have your kids thinking and running as quickly as the tide can move.

—*From the Author*

---

ings, it is best to choose a neutral meeting place, such as a playground, where the adults can talk and get to know each other while keeping an eye on the kids. Don't pick a potentially crowded or busy place, such as the zoo, for the first few times, since that could make conversation difficult. After you get to know the other members, then you have the choice of continuing to meet in neutral places or opening it up to people's houses. How big can a group get? Stillwell reports that D.C. Metro Dads now boasts ninety-three members in three chapters in the Northern Virginia area.

And do you always have to meet in the same place and do the same thing? No. Art Margolis of Menlo Park, New Jersey (formerly of California), reports that in one month his group went to a science center, the Natural History Museum in New York City, and the Barnum and Bailey Circus. Michael Hunsinger, who runs a playgroup in Rifle, Colorado, has enjoyed going to parks, pools, hiking, and on nature walks. Of his San Diego group, Jim DiCenzo reports, "We made a trip up to the mountains, about an hour northeast of San Diego, to play in the snow. We all had a great time throwing snowballs, sled-riding, and making snowmen."

A newsletter or Web site can help keep your group organized. Here you can post all meeting times and events. One dad who has had great success creating his own newsletter is Peter Hoh from Bloomington, Minnesota, the publisher of the *Minnesota Dads At Home Newsletter*. "You don't have to be a desktop publishing professional, an experienced writer, or a computer wizard to get started," he says. "It helps to have willing volunteers and a clear sense of purpose. As you recruit volunteers you may find some people who have experience. If experienced members cannot make a regular commitment to help with the newsletter, ask if they are willing to serve as a resource for the less experienced volunteers. This sort of mentorship builds relationships within the group.

"Now our eight-page newsletter is bimonthly, with a calendar of events on a separate sheet. On the off months we simply mail the single-sheet calendar of events." Some newsletter departments to consider that Hoh recommends are feature articles, commentary/opinion pieces, profiles of at-home dads and playgroups, a cooking column, an advice column, and reviews of places to go with your kids, such as playgrounds or museums.

If you do not have the resources to put out a newsletter, you can simply put out a one-page calendar each month to pass out to your members at the playground or your meeting place of choice. You will find that some dads who initially show interest may not show up at future meetings, but if you continue to send them a calendar of events in the mail or through e-mail, you may find them showing up at a future event.

Dads' Night Out

Curtis Cooper of Shawnee, Kansas, who started his own group called DAD-to-DAD, which helps organize playgroups, came up with the idea of a monthly night out for the dads who attended his playgroups. (DAD-to-DAD is now part of the At-Home Dad Network; see the resource section for more information.) Playgroup leader Casey Spencer notes that his popular nights out include dinner, bowling, or a trip to a batting cage or go-kart track. He advises that a good schedule to follow is once a month on weeknights.

Organizers should give time for the dads' wives to come home and take over. Other suggestions include:

- Remember to check your night-out destinations, the same as any other event: check directions, reservation policies, and prices, and try not to go to a place on its busiest night. Dinners may last up to two hours.
- I suggest you give your wife a lot of advance notice. On her night at home while you play, she should know that you appreciate the freedom.
- Plan a weekend family event. If you stop to think about it, some of us give a lot of lip service to the uniqueness of our role. Whether we're whining or bragging, we sometimes forget that our wives are in just as unique a situation. It can be comforting for the breadwinners to find out that they aren't alone, either. At some point, survey your members to see if a weekend family event is a good idea. These give new participants a chance to get involved and can lead to lasting whole-family friendships.

So the best thing to do is find a way to keep in touch and then keep it going.

Hanging Out with the Moms

Just because you feel more comfortable with the idea of bonding with men than you do with women does not mean you should shun the moms forever. Dads often feel very uncomfortable trying to fit in with at-home moms. James Sulanowski, from Cranston, Rhode Island, met up with one mom one day at a bagel shop with his four-month-old, Emily. He says he picked the bagel shop because "it offered the safety valve of an activity (eating bagels), unlike sitting in the park, where it's harder to avoid an unwanted conversation."

Pointed Table Talk

A fun way to spend your dinnertime is to have a table manners contest. Here's the point system. For comments made or actions taken during dinner:

- "Please" or "Thank you" = 1 point
- Using forks, not fingers = 1 point
- Saying "No, thank you" = 1 point
- Keeping legs under table = 2 points
- Saying "Excuse me" when done = 2 points
- Not talking with your mouth full = 2 points
- Not interrupting = 2 points
- Taking little bites = 2 points
- Complimenting each other = 3 points

When they get a point, announce it to all and keep a running total in your head. This is fun, and although it will get out of hand with the "please's" and "thank you's" flying around, it's a blast and it gets a message across.

—From the Author

At least at a bagel shop, you won't be outnumbered ten to one, as you may be in a playground surrounded by mothers.

Randy Brown of Frederick, Maryland, has also turned to women for support. He says,

It was rare to find another man doing this househusband thing, so for me it was natural to seek out women with kids in the same age range as mine. That wasn't too hard. I got good feedback and support, and think about it: if you need help with something, doesn't it make sense to go to the experts? I mean, what are you going to learn from another dad about cooking, cleaning, nurturing, scheduling, PTA etiquette, and so forth, that you couldn't learn better from a woman who loves doing it, was trained to do it right, and has an elaborate support network?

By working together and learning from stay-at-home moms, you can improve the quality of your days.

Some of the mothers you meet at the playground and other meeting places may be ill at ease with a man in their midst, but you need to keep being friendly and make yourself familiar to them so they will become comfortable. David Boylan of Chicago decided to face the moms head-on by signing up for a Mom & Tot gym and swim class with his daughter, Caitlin. Boylan says being in this class helped break down the barrier

> because the mothers saw me diaper my kid the way they diaper theirs. I looked for every opportunity to help out in a non-threatening way, with an extra diaper, some powder, and No More Tangles hair spray. After sticking my nose into the circle of moms having their daily conversations, they came to accept me.

Remember that these women are your coworkers, so try not to feel intimidated by them.

While you may be feeling a little proud and maybe a bit defensive at being the only at-home dad you know, do not try too hard when first engaging moms in conversations. Stick to what you know, and admit to what you don't. For example, opening a conversation on the topic of clothes may not be the best idea unless you have a great sense of style, which frankly I find is never the case with at-home dads. The reality is that if our kids' clothes match, it's a coincidence. Some easy topics to start a conversation are: "Does he go to preschool?" or "What other playgrounds would you recommend for kids?" Don't be afraid to appeal to mothers for suggestions. If you see that a mother's child is playing with a new kind of toy that you have been thinking of getting, ask about it and find out where she bought the toy.

While confidence and persistence are key, patience may be even more important. Moms, who are sometimes already suspicious of the one man in the playground, might misinterpret your eagerness as something else. Although I got some strange looks, I made it a point to start up a conversation with whoever was sitting next to me on the sandbox. Once they saw my son was well cared for, they realized that I wasn't some nut on parole or some fiend trying to make time with them, and they then ended up being very helpful. It didn't take long before we would quickly pass the small talk on how old our kids were and settle down and compare notes on naps, blankies, bottles, and sippy cups.

One good piece of advice that I have picked up over the years is to look for the moms on the weekends, when they are with their husbands, and then focus on their husbands. Peter Hoh found that the relationship with the moms is better if you strike up a conversation with the husband first. "Once the dad gets to know you, he'll realize that you are a henpecked wuss and not after his wife." Also, by meeting moms on weekends, when you are with your wife, you can offset any potential concerns that you are interested in more than what kind of diapers they prefer.

Play Dates

Along with becoming the primary caregiver comes the added role of being your child's personal assistant. With sports practice, music lessons, tutoring, endless birthdays, and playtimes with others, you may be surprised at what a busy social calendar your kids have. While it's a lot for a parent to keep up with, it also provides a wealth of opportunities for you to meet other parents. Ask your children if there are any nice kids with whom they want to set up a play date, and call the parents to set it up. You can use this as an excuse to invite the parents over or to wherever the date is—this can give you some one-on-one time with adults.

Similarly, taking your kids to birthday parties and sports practices and hanging out for a while will give you the chance to meet other parents. One great thing about being a parent is that you will already have some commonalities to talk about, and you can use your kids as a starting point. Teachers are also a great resource here. If you want to set up a play date with some kids whose primary caregivers are dads, just ask your kids' teachers whom you should call. They will be happy to help.

Arts and Crafts

Here are some ideas for hands-on fun.

- Try finger painting with corn syrup that has a few drops of food coloring added. The drops of food coloring make the pictures very shiny, pretty, and cool-looking when they dry. It may be a bit messy, but the kids love it!
- Try making homemade butter. Fill clean baby food jars half full with whipping cream, seal the lids tightly, and shake like mad for five minutes. Pour off the liquid (whey), add a pinch of salt, and enjoy on crackers.
- Here's a great bubble-making recipe: 1 cup (230 mL) water, 1/3 cup (80 mL) liquid dish soap, and 1 tablespoon (14.8 mL) corn syrup.
- Develop early cutting skills by letting your little ones cut up cooked spaghetti.

—*Peter Horn, Wauwatosa, Wisconsin*

Connecting with the Internet

Every Monday night at 10 P.M., David Boylan of Chicago holds online meetings with up to twenty at-home dads across the country. During one hot night last summer, Boylan arrived first in the "shade tree" message board, ready to lead the group of dads logged onto their computers across the country on a chat about summer activities for kids. (A chat room can be found on a Web site, or via an online service provider such as America Online [AOL]), where people can communicate to each other by typing out messages using a computer keyboard. The typed text appears instantly on the other chat room members' monitors, so it's very much like talking with others.) As they slowly gathered together, one dad talks about separation anxiety, another about a house move, and a third brags that his daughter is now climbing the stairs. Boylan quickly takes up the subject at hand. He asks, "How many folks have to deal with the ice cream truck? My kids go bonkers when the truck comes around." The dads chime in with suggestions on hot weather tips they've used. An egg cream with ice cream on top, root beer floats, sprinklers, the kiddie pool, an air-conditioned library. Boylan then relates to the others how he "caught my kids standing in the open refrigerator last week just to cool off." Suddenly, a mom (anyone can log in and join in on a public chat) pops in the chat room and quickly excuses herself as she notes that the room is filled with dads. Boylan encourages her to stay, and she joins in the chat.

Mark Baron of Sharon, Massachusetts, initiates a flurry of activity by asking, "How well do things go with squirt bottle fights?" Again the dads chime in. One shouts, "Super soakers! . . . Dad gets the hose . . . serious watergun fight!" He recommends to "Stake out a spot near the refill bucket." Another dad, an authority on the subject, says, "The one with the backpack is the best . . . you look like the Orkin Man with that thing!" What makes this chat so extraordinary is that all dads and moms at this meeting are in their respective homes typing their comments on their computers while their kids are safely tucked into bed.

Boylan, looking to meet other at-home dads for conversations, turned to his computer and started this weekly chat from his Chicago home in the mid-1990s. It was the first chat group about at-home dads on AOL. Using AOL, he named his group the "Stay-At Home/Primary Care Dads Chat." Dave, like many new at-home fathers, turned to the Internet to find others like him. Upon finding the communities on AOL, he states, "I was blown away by the opportunities for entertainment and communication. In my heart, I genuinely believed no one was out there. I can't tell you how excited I got when I saw postings to the folder!!! And they were saying, 'I'm glad to find this folder. I thought I was the only one!' "

You can find dad chat rooms on any major Internet provider; you just need to do a simple search in their sites to join them or start your own.

One of the older at-home dad message boards (started September 1998) is run by Hal Levy of Manalapan, New Jersey, and is called the DadsList on Yahoo! Here you can receive up to thirty e-mails a day (or get all of them in one shot once a day). Levy has had great success with his list, noting, "I remember one father who gave a portion of his liver to his son. We raised some meager funds and sent him e-mails to cheer him up. He was really happy that the stay-at-home dads came together and helped in the ways they could." Levy describes his board as a place where there is "a party going on and anyone is invited."

Marty Josephson of Milwaukee, Wisconsin, has one of the most successful and active online chat rooms with his Dads-at-Home message board on Yahoo! He notes,

> We have had some dads in the Northwest who have arranged a camping trip, some dads in the Midwest who are going to a Cubs game, and some dads who have hooked up when visiting each other's communities. I have found using the Internet to be a great source of feedback on things I am feeling, and a very effective way of venting when the kids are driving

me crazy. However, while going online can provide some sense of relief from the isolation you are experiencing, be careful of letting it take over your life.

Indeed, Chris Stafford of Brighton, Minnesota, the original founder of *Full-Time Dads* magazine, warns, "Far too many at-home fathers spend excessive amounts of time sitting at the computers 'enhancing' their lives, at the expense of their children."

Dryer Lint Modeling

You must try this one!

Dryer lint modeling compound ingredients
3 cups (700 mL) dryer lint
2 cups (460 mL) cold water
⅔ cup (160 mL) flour
3 drops oil of wintergreen
old newspaper

In a large pan, place lint and water and stir to dampen all parts of the lint. Add flour and stir well, being careful to prevent lumps. Add the oil of wintergreen and stir well. Cook over low heat, stirring constantly, until mixture holds together and forms peaks. Pour out onto several thicknesses of old newspaper to cool. This makes about 4 cups (1 liter). You can store this in an airtight container when not in use. The consistency will be moldable like modeling clay when it cools off. You can use this to shape over boxes, balloons, or even press it into a mold. It will take three to five days to dry.

—Ray DeGolia, Orange County, California

Other Suggestions to Help You Connect

At the 2003 At-Home Dad Convention held in Chicago, I questioned attendees on what they have done to help with isolation besides forming playgroups. Some of the dads actually *enjoyed* their time alone or were lucky enough to have friends or neighbors who have kids that are the same age with whom they could spend time. Many dads needed to make more of an effort to connect with people, and they offered these simple survival tips that have worked for them:

- Go for walks and try to meet neighbors of all ages. Introduce yourself to parents with kids.
- Keep in contact with regular friends and old coworkers with visits or calls.
- Volunteer with an ambulance service, homeless shelter, and more.
- Join the YMCA, a swimming club, or a church group.
- Get involved with your children's school—join the PTA or be a teacher's aid, safety patrol, or field trip chaperone.
- Some museums are free a few days of the week. Also try the zoo, mall, or even sitting in a bookstore.
- Play basketball with a church or community group.
- Work part-time at your old job.

I end this chapter below with one dad who started a new approach in playgroups and was able to take his idea nationwide. I hope this chapter has given you new ideas on connecting with new dads. In the next chapter I will help examine many at-home dads' first worry: "How will we survive on one income?"

SPOTLIGHT ON DAD

"One Dad's Story of Starting a Playgroup," a profile of Curtis Cooper

BY PETER BAYLIES   *Curtis Cooper now lives in Shawnee, Kansas. His organization, DAD-to-DAD, sponsors many playgroups in the At-Home Dad Network. Please check www.athomedad.com for more information.*

Curtis Cooper, living in Atlanta, Georgia, at the time, ran into the problem of isolation when he became a stay-at-home dad to his newborn son, Brett. Wanting to avoid daycare for their son, he and his wife, Pam, agreed that Pam had the better career and salary potential, and so the decision for Curtis to stay home with his son was easy. The hard part was finding other dads with whom to connect. Cooper notes, "When I became a stay-at-home dad, like most of us, I wasn't quite sure what it would be like. I found myself feeling pretty isolated and insecure at first, and missed the daily interaction with my friends and coworkers." Unable to find dads right away, he joined some of the moms on his street every other week. Although he enjoyed it, he felt "a little out of place."

He then decided to start a playgroup for dads, and gave it the name Mr. Mom Club. (After a few meetings and checking with his friends, the title was quickly scrapped for the more appropriate DAD-to-DAD.) He put a few ads in the local papers and, with only two dads calling back, he started a group that has met weekly since then. As word of Cooper's efforts spread via an article in the *Atlanta Constitution* newspaper and word of mouth, dads kept showing up. It got to the point where Cooper had contact with more than thirty stay-at-home dads in the Atlanta area. So many, in fact, that he had to set up two chapters to handle the load.

Adding a new twist to the playgroup idea, he started a Dads-Night-Out dinner (without the kids), which meets every two to three weeks at restaurants in the local area. Andy Doetsch, one of the first to join, and the head of a local chapter in Alpharetta, Georgia, says,

"Some weeks, I live for the Dads-Night-Out dinners. It's important for sanity's sake, bouncing ideas off the other dads, getting input from them as to how they might handle certain situations that have come up, and more. I think the most important things I have gotten from the group are the friendships that have developed, the camaraderie of people who are doing the same thing I am and who aren't afraid to 'go against the norm' or ignore the stereotypes floating around about primary caregivers."

A peek at a recent DAD-to-DAD schedule shows many activities to keep the dads and kids busy:

SEPTEMBER 12:   North Point Mall, Kids Club. Meet at the merry-go-round between 10 and 10:30 A.M.

SEPTEMBER 14:   Alpharetta Library (which offered a storytime just for DAD-to-DAD).

SEPTEMBER 18:   Dads-Night-Out dinner at 7:30 P.M. at Rafters in Alpharetta.

SEPTEMBER 19:   Cooper is hosting a playgroup at 10 A.M.

SEPTEMBER 26:   Atlanta Zoo. Meet at the playground inside the zoo at 10 A.M.

A short time later, Cooper decided to try to expand DAD-to-DAD into a national organization, and sent out press releases to the media. Soon, CNN and *ABC World News Tonight* came knocking at his door. Cooper had to get used to the cameras whirring and lights blazing as the dads talked of sports and the kids happily played during their field trips to the zoo.

Within a few months, Cooper was able to get readers of the *At-Home Dad Newsletter* to start new DAD-to-DAD chapters in Arizona, Massachusetts, Virginia, North and South Carolina, Kansas, and Minnesota. Scott Hahn, a chapter leader in Richmond, Virginia, says,

> Slowly but surely, the Richmond chapter is getting underway. Today we
> will have our third playgroup activity. Next Tuesday we will have our
> second Dads-Night-Out dinner. My daughter and I were alone at the

first playgroup meeting. We were joined by a dad and two other kids for the second. Three dads (including me) attended the first dinner.

Hahn is now in contact with ten other at-home dads who publicized their activities in the local media and neighborhood newsletters to reach more people. He is hoping to set up a few chapters in the Richmond area so that everyone can join DAD-to-DAD activities without a long drive.

Of the playgroups, Cooper notes, "Starting a playgroup isn't easy, but it's one of the most rewarding things I've ever done. The friends I've made through DAD-to-DAD are some of my best." Doetsch agrees, adding,

> I really enjoy getting together for playgroup every week with the other dads in our chapter. My children (Christian, 5, and Kayla, 2½) have gotten to know several of the other children in the group and have fun getting together with them, sometimes several times a week. Through DAD-to-DAD, I have become good friends with another dad who lives right around the corner from me. It's also nice to know there is a babysitter who can be available in emergencies!

5

Living on One Income

When I started my stint as an at-home dad, the biggest worry that kept me up at night was, "How are we going to survive on one income?" On paper, losing my entire salary—half of our family income—did not look feasible. It seemed to be an impossible amount of money to lose, and it wasn't clear we could cover all our expenses without this money. Like many parents, I thought the only way I could stay home was if I had a nice cash reserve. A check of the Microsoft Money Web site (http://moneycentral.msn.com), which provides estimates for the costs of raising a child depending on income, seemed to confirm my thoughts. The figures were staggering: the cost of raising a child from birth to seventeen years of age ranged from $124,000 for a $39K income to $249,000 for a $69K+ income. If a news journalist took the highest figure and rounded it off, he could create a frightening headline, such as: "$250,000 Needed to Raise One Child." That fact can scare any dad enough to stay in his cubicle, especially if he has more than one child. But do you really need a half million to raise a couple of kids? This didn't ring true for me.

It seems that these surprisingly high expenses of raising children also didn't ring true for at-home dad Jim Chapa of Downers Grove, Illinois. After taking a closer look at these figures, he realized that the savings associated with not going to work every day outweighed the costs of childcare. Below are Chapa's numbers on the cost of working. With these numbers in hand, he suggested that the title of this chapter should be, "How can you afford to live on two incomes?"

> Put together a simple spreadsheet. Daycare for two kids, nine hours a day at, what, $10 an hour? That's $450 a week, times, say, fifty weeks in a work year. That amounted to $22,500. OK, now you need a more dependable car for work. That is $350 a month, plus additional insurance, plus the extra gas (not even getting into wear-and-tear depreciation). That ends up to be about $5K a year. Appropriate business clothes? Another $1K a year. Lunch at work? Even if you only spend $3 a day extra, that's $750 a year. According to my calculations, that's about $29,000. Not to mention additional medical expenses, sick days, and all of the other "throw your kids in daycare" costs. But wait, there's more! If you're spending $29,000 just to go to work, you need to make another $11K, just to pay the federal, state, and local taxes to bring home $29,000. ($40,000 per year, taxed at .28% = $28,800 take-home). So, it costs around $40,000 in pretax dollars just to break even when sending two kids into childcare, just so you can "go to work." As always, your mileage may vary. Then, add in the social expense of having your children raised by strangers.

Take a look at Chapa's figures and apply them to yourself, and you might be surprised to see the cost-effectiveness of staying at home.

Other dads have been convinced by their wives to stay home because of the high costs associated with both parents going to full-time jobs. Joyce Strong of Springfield, Massachusetts, who works at home, convinced her husband to quit his job, because

> I determined that it was actually more expensive for him to go to work outside of the house. I'm a mom who works at home. I have five children and I've been working from home

for about ten years. When my fourth child was born, I found that many things I used to hire people to do, we could now do ourselves much more cheaply. We eliminated many expenses altogether, including daycare, a housekeeper, take-out food because now we had more time to plan and cook, landscaping, commuting costs, clothing costs (I can work in my PJs), etc. I know that I can save much more money by having time to be a more thoughtful consumer with more time to plan and more time to use my imagination.

See the resources listed in the back of this book for good books on ways to save money.

Winter Beach Party

Surprise your wife and kids with a vacation to the Bahamas without leaving the house! Prepare to go to the beach, but instead of loading up the car, just put on your bathing suits and set it up in your own living room. Here are the supplies you'll need:

    towels
    bucket of sand
    beach chairs
    cooler filled with food
    sunglasses

You can make a dinner fit for the beach, too, with lobsters (if there's room in your budget for this, or fish sticks if not), steamers, and tropical drinks. Play the best of the Beach Boys' music and enjoy. If you are actually planning a trip, get the vacation catalogs and plan it with the family during your indoor party (no suntan lotion needed).
    —*Kenneth Donovan, North Andover, Massachusetts*

In this chapter you will read about several dads who have successfully saved money at home. I will examine how people think about money and look at ways to cut corners. For example, instead of trucking your kids to Chuck E. Cheese's, you can consider free resources in your own town. I'll also examine how your kids can have fun on rainy days with what you already have in your house. Finally, I will share ideas about yard sales, eBay, and home repairs as further ways to save money.

Changing Your State of Mind and Adjusting Your Lifestyle

In order to save money, you need to address your standard-of-living expectations and take into account how your parents spent money on you as a child. Also, you need to figure out what sacrifices you want to make to achieve your goal of spending less. Bob Higgins of St. Cloud, Florida, says,

> I think it has a lot to do with how people were raised, and how people differentiate between "needs" and "wants." I think lots of people get into what I'll call a "cycle of debt." When you've done without or lived on a fixed income and suddenly have what seems like much more because of a second income, most people will go out and buy stuff on credit, not realizing that they are inadvertently locking themselves into "needing" that second income. What was a "luxury" becomes a must-have. Many parents will also do what they think is a great thing and go out and blow all kinds of money on stuff for the kids. They don't realize that kids don't "need" all of the PlayStations, etc. Sure, we all want to give our kids some material goods, but the only thing they really need (naturally, other than food and clothes), is a parent or parents who are attentive, who are loving/caring, and who are around and willing to answer questions.

Higgins explains how he and his wife have learned how to pick and choose what "wants" they are willing to splurge on, and which ones are out of their league. For example, he doesn't mind ordering the most expensive steak on the menu, but since he doesn't go out much, it doesn't matter. Could he go out and buy a new boat or truck? Probably, but, as he says, "When I think about how often I'm going to actually need a truck or how often we're going to use a boat, and then when I think about the fact that the truck will put us back to the tune of probably $25K, I see that we don't need that."

By assessing his wants and needs, Higgins is able to think ahead and save some money. One budget buster is impulse buying, which is caused by no or too little thinking! The next time you feel you "need" to purchase an item, ask yourself these questions before following through:

- Do you want this item or do you need it? If you don't need it, simply don't buy it. If you have any doubt, sleep on it.
- If after sleeping on it you decide you do need it, ask yourself how long can you wait until you have to buy this item. If you can wait a few weeks, then ask yourself the next two questions.
- How can you get what you need at the cheapest price?
- Can you get this item used?

Now you can avoid the impulsive decision by taking your time, reassessing your needs, and comparison shopping either in the classifieds or online.

Adding on to the Savings at Home

At home you will find more ways to add on to the savings you have automatically made by leaving work. For example, automatic sav-

---

Fast-Food Cloning

Make your hamburgers taste like they were freshly made at a fast-food place. Use the cheap, thin generic-brand buns (the type you can easily poke a hole in). Then take the top of a round Tupperware container about 5 inches round, press the hamburger flat, and cook it. Here's the crucial step: mix two parts ketchup, one part mustard, and spread on top of the hamburger. This gives it that secret barbecue flavor the kids seem to love. They won't know the difference, except they won't get a toy. (If your child doesn't recognize a meal without a toy with it, get an old, tiny, plastic toy that he's forgotten about from the cellar, slip it into a baggie, and serve.)

—From the Author

---

ings can come by way of your car. Jim Chapa notes, "Since I don't drive forty-five minutes to work every day, I can afford to drive an old car. I'll take my '90 Land Cruiser over any car under $30K today. Not to mention the savings in taxes, insurance, and depreciation." Mike Donahue of San Francisco, California, father of ten-year-old Ryan, seventeen-month-old Sean, and two-month-old Mackenzie, cuts expenses further.

> My wife, Nancy, cuts my hair, and together, we cut the younger kids' hair. I can't remember when we've bought a pizza or fast food, but we make our own types of pizzas and different dinners. The older kids each have their favorites that we try to work in, and we all try to help in food prep and cleanup (it's more fun). I do the kids' meals during the days . . . mostly during the week (sometimes Nancy won't get home until after 8 P.M.). I'm not paying for lunches, not even a few times per week. We have many in-laws who have chil-

dren who are slightly older and have given us lots of items and clothes.

Think about ways you can similarly incorporate savings—and fun—into your routine.

When I started as an at-home dad, I made it my new goal in life (other than to be a fabulous parent and husband) to increase our savings. If I could not bring in money as an at-home dad, I decided that I would take it upon myself to make sure we were saving wherever we could. In my experiences, I have found four major areas where dads can save the most money:

- Kid expenses
- Shopping at yard sales or on eBay
- Doing repairs yourself
- Shopping for bargains

I will explore each of these items below.

Kid Fun: Free Activities That Will Save You Money— and Not Skimp on the Fun

When I watch home movies of myself as a kid, I see the memories that I treasure most: digging in the sand at the beach with my parents, or getting up on Dad's shoulders to pick apples. It is these simple activities and games I did with my parents that I remember best. I can't remember one thing that sticks out as a memory that required spending money. There are plenty of companies ready, willing, and able to do the thinking for you when it comes to creating fun experiences for kids (Chuck E. Cheese's, Disneyland). But you don't always have to spend money to entertain your kids. With my two kids, I have tried to let my imagination do more of the work than my wallet. Here's a list of eleven easy activities that require nothing except your time. You, no doubt, will think of plenty more:

1. *Visit the local pet store.* It's closer than the zoo and it's free. Then head to the library and pick out a book on a favorite animal. And if you live near a zoo, enjoy the animals there, too. Check to see if a zoo near you offers discounted entrance fees on certain days.

2. *Go to the library.* Speaking of the library, this is also a great resource—as opposed to a bookstore—for you to visit with your kids. It's also a good way to help them learn about responsibility by providing them with a library card and putting them in charge of getting the books back on time.

3. *Get out your old clothes.* You can clean out your closet and keep your kids happy by letting them try "dressing up" with the oversized clothes. You will be surprised how long this will keep them happy. (It's pretty funny to watch, too.) You can also organize a garage sale to sell your old clothes and other items post–spring cleaning to make a little extra money and cut down on the clutter in your home.

4. *Set up an obstacle course.* Use old boxes, tables, and chairs that kids can tunnel through. Try a variation: have them carry spoonfuls of Cheerios through the maze.

5. *Make a store.* If you have a large box in the basement, drag it out and cut a large hole in front to serve as a play store. Kids can get inside and set up their wares to sell—maybe you can even collect empty food boxes to stock a play grocery store. Have the kids make up a name for their business (and even write prices on the items if they are old enough); this is a fun way to teach counting skills.

6. *Recyclable Legos.* Save your recyclable goods such as paper towel/toilet paper tubes, egg cartons, plastic containers, old magazines, and even your junk mail. Keep it all in a big box, toss it on the floor, and let your kids' imaginations take over. You'll be surprised what kids can do with "junk."

7. *Make modeling clay.* Mix together 1 cup (230 mL) of flour, ½ (115 mL) cup of salt, 2 teaspoons (9.8 mL) cream of tartar, 1

cup (230 mL) of water, 1 tablespoon (14.8 mL) of oil, and 4 drops of food coloring. Combine all ingredients in a saucepan, cook over medium heat, stirring constantly until it forms a ball. Continue cooking until it's not sticky to touch. Let it cool, and then play! Store in an airtight container and it will remain usable. Once it's out in the air for an extended period of time, however, the mixture hardens and becomes useless.

8. *Peanut butter bird feeder.* Take a pinecone, roll it in peanut butter, then roll it in birdseed and hang it on a tree. You and your children can watch from a distance and try to identify the birds that enjoy your crafty treat. You can either search for the type of bird you saw with your child via the Internet (or a library book), or you can suggest that your kids try to create a picture of the bird that they witnessed visiting the pinecone.

9. *Read Dr. Seuss's* Green Eggs and Ham. And then in the morning make it for breakfast using green food coloring.

10. *Cookie cutter lunch.* Use a cookie cutter to cut out bread and meat and cheese into fun shapes, and then eat your art for lunch. Pile them up for a fun sandwich. Try it with pancakes, too!

11. *Choo-choo boxcar train.* Make a choo-choo train by tying together those cardboard boxes you have in the basement and give those million stuffed animals in your kids' bed a ride around the house. You can punch a small hole in the boxes and use string, rope, or even a bungee cord to attach them together.

In addition to these ideas, you may have a few ideas of your own to try with the kids. Sometimes I will pull out old baby toys my kids may not have played with in a while and pile them on the floor. I was surprised at how much fun they had digging through their memories, saying, "Remember when we used to play with these?" Also, don't be afraid to check out a few of the numerous "things to do with kids" books from the library. These books are filled with everything from magic tricks and card games to cook-

Hot Summer Kid Tips

Here are some additional fun tips to help you and your kids enjoy the summer:

- Freeze a toy in a gallon jug, cut the plastic off, and put it in the toddler pool. Your kids will have fun watching it melt in the sun and water.
- Fill a paper cup with water, place it on top of your child's head, and race him or her across the yard. If you have more than one child, you can hold the stopwatch and they can race each other. See if your children can shorten the time it takes to cross the yard.
- Water balloon or wet sponge toss! Have two kids or yourself and your child stand one foot apart from each other and throw the balloon or sponge, then move back a foot at a time to see how far you can throw it without dropping or, in the case of the water balloon, breaking it. When they are done with the sponge, have a car washing party (radio needed).
- Ice cube meltdown in armpit! This is a fun one, and you can do it with one child or several. Just have them stand in place and put ice cubes under their armpits to see who can hold it there the longest. Sit back and watch them dance!
- Create an obstacle course. Set up some plastic sand buckets or even cups of water in a line, with room to move in between. In turn, time each kid as he runs in a zigzag fashion between the cups, without knocking them over. You can do a second turn rapidly walking backward.
- Have a watermelon seed spitting contest.
- If you have a big, unused piece of plywood, rest it against your garage and allow creative painting.

— From the Author

ing and crafts. From these, you will be able to pick out a few age-appropriate things to try out with your kids.

Shopping at Yard Sales and on eBay

With my new mission to increase family savings, I first focused on how to cut down on our children's expenses. My initial idea was to keep my kids away from the stores. When the kids were younger, I shopped at night, and they basically never saw the inside of a supermarket (and *never* a toy store). But by far the best way for my wife and me to save money is to shop at yard sales. We can pick up good-quality clothes (kids outgrow clothes more quickly than they get wear-and-tear . . . sometimes) and toys at ten cents on the dollar, or even at no charge from the free box. In the warm months we go to yard sales with the kids. When we go to yard sales and buy an item, say a Lego set for $5, I explain to them that it would cost $49.99 in the store and have them figure out how much money they save. This way they learn a little bit about math and finances in the process.

Another way that I find shopping at yard sales helpful is to buy Christmas and birthday presents in advance. I just store them away to avoid the last-minute holiday/birthday present rush, when budgets can get crushed by your holiday spirit.

In the summer, on Saturday mornings I call out, "Who wants to shop for toys?" And my two boys come running. By the time we get home after a day of garage sale shopping, the kids have a collection of Lincoln Logs, Transformers, Legos, and maybe a few things from the free box. This is usually enough to keep them entertained for at least a few weeks. And the best part about it: if the toys break or if my kids get sick of a toy quickly, then it doesn't hurt so much.

At-home dad Jerry Culbertson of Scottsburg, Indiana, had particularly good luck buying clothes for his child one summer. "I bought bibs and jackets, quality winter wear in excellent condition for $1 each. They would have cost around $75 to $100 new. They will eventually go to my granddaughter."

In addition to going to yard sales, we like to have one ourselves now and then. It's a good way to clean out the house and make a few bucks at the same time. When I told the kids they could keep the money from their stuff, they spent a week cleaning up the basement looking for every toy they had outgrown. When we told our neighbors about the sale, we found out a few wanted to join in. We ended up having a multi-yard sale and shared a classified ad. For us it was great, the kids loved it, the house was cleaner, and we made about $100 (instead of spending it on an activity we might have done instead).

If you are uncomfortable having yard sales or going to them, eBay is a great second choice in buying and selling new and used items. Over the years, eBay has become a dominant and trusted online source for auctions. You can see pictures of the exact goods that are for sale and bid on them against other eBay shoppers for a specified time (determined by the seller). Also, before you buy an item, you can check the seller's feedback. Here you can see how buyers have provided positive, neutral, or negative responses to the seller, complete with comments. To buy an item, you just need to register an account on www.eBay.com. If you want to sell, however, you need to give them your credit card number. The big downside of buying items on eBay are the shipping costs, which can cut into some of the savings. Clothing for children is a good buy, as are videos and toys. I know one woman who bought her daughter a snowsuit for $20. (While you can get good deals on eBay, I find that yard sales are still cheaper, but it depends where you live and how much time you are willing to put into shopping at them.)

I have used eBay to sell several items that I probably would have otherwise thrown away. For example, clothes that your kids have grown out of or their old toys seem to get a higher price on eBay than in yard sales. My most extraordinary example of an eBay sale involved my 1989 Buick Century, which was in such bad shape I had trouble giving it away. When I started it up, the smoke nearly filled the neighborhood as I drove it down the street. Each school day the

Sand Castles

To make sand castles that last forever, mix together 2 cups (460 mL) of sand, 1 cup (230 mL) of cornstarch, and 1 cup (230 mL) of water. Keep this on the stove until the consistency becomes like a thick pudding. Allow it to cool. Your kids can use it like modeling clay; when allowed to dry, it will be as hard as a rock. Add shells, buttons, and feathers for decorations.

—*Sue Baylies, North Andover, Massachusetts*

kids would try to guess if it would start up that morning. Finally, I called a towing company, and even they didn't want it. I put an ad in the classifieds and advertised it as free for anyone who would take it. But those that showed up even passed on it. Then, on a whim, I checked eBay and found that some of the parts were actually worth something. The most valuable was the taillight, which fit Buick Century models 1989–1996. I listed it and seven days later received twenty-two bids for a final price of $170. I ended up selling the headlights for another $40 and gave away my radio and battery to a few neighbors. After letting my kids and some of their friends have fun tearing apart the car, I finally found another towing company that would take it for free, even with the parts missing.

Sweat Equity: Doing Your Own Home Repairs

When I was a full-time working parent, I relied on contractors to do even the simplest repairs around the home, such as unclogging a toilet. I had no time to do it myself, and frankly, I didn't know how. I didn't know how to change the oil in my car, either. But when a simple repair on your toilet can cost $40 just for the house call, this can motivate you pretty quick to learn how to do it yourself. With a vast amount of how-to information available on the

Internet or at your local library, you can look up nearly all the common repairs and construction ideas for your home.

Since I've made the choice to be home, I learned how to replace a dryer belt, replace my own windows, install my dishwasher, fix minor leaks in the toilet, and even renovate my garage into a family room. The family room project started with an old, unfinished garage that had a cracked cement floor and a slightly bowed roof. A contractor could do the job for around $20,000. Where to start? Well, the first thing you have to do is get a permit from the town's building inspector. Don't be afraid to ask him for tips—he can also lead you to some of the reputable contractors in town. I learned more by asking these contractors how they would do the job. I peppered them with questions and received advice that has saved me quite a bit of time and money. Over an eight-month period, I taught myself how to install a plywood base over the existing cracked cement floor, install electric wiring and plugs, do dry wall, straighten out a bowed roof (yuck!), put in insulation, install carpeting over the plywood base, and install a ceiling fan. With a search of the classifieds, I was able to get used windows for cheap, and I even retrieved a free bay window from a neighbor who was ready to throw it away. The knowledge I gained helped me with other, smaller projects, too. And it will continue to help me save money over the years. In fact, I promised my (very patient) wife that my next project would be to remodel the bathroom—when this book is complete. So I hope by the time you are reading this we have a bathroom that doesn't look like a bomb shelter covered with soap scum.

"I really had no idea how to do most of this house maintenance stuff," says at-home dad Mike Donahue, who like me, started out with no experience.

> I used to hand my dad wrenches and watch (and help) him. My father-in-law is also very handy. I guess I really just jumped in to try to do this on my own. I used the Internet

and the home improvement TV shows for guidance and made sure I had an extra wax ring for a toilet. I eventually learned how to do many of the repairs myself. I'm sure I made many mistakes, but I learned a lot and had a blast (most of the time). We're on well water, and it seems our pipes spring leaks at the most inconvenient times. I watched the repairman once and asked him questions and have since managed to fix the new leaks. This past Christmas Eve, our ten-year-old, Ryan, told us that the upstairs toilet was "not flushing very well." I went up and plunged for about five minutes, and nothing. I ended up removing the toilet and discovered three pacifiers and my shaving blade holder were all stuck in it. We pinned it on Sean, my youngest son. I ran up to a local Super Wal-Mart and got too many parts, along with a few wax rings. (Luckily, we had an additional bathroom.) I put the toilet back the day after Christmas without a hitch and didn't mess up the wax ring (the extra is still good). We've learned to keep the doors shut now, since my son Sean is mobile.

Jim Chapa has gone beyond minor home repair. While at home, he has made a living renovating houses and selling them for a profit. How does he do it while home with the kids? Simple. He lives in

---

Baby Echo Machine

While yelling upstairs one day to see if my son was there, I noticed an echo sound in the receiving end of our baby monitor. My son got a kick out of making the effect by trying the same thing. He learned a little about sound waves and how fast they travel (one mile in five seconds).

—From the Author

the house while he's working on it. By improving a home, he adds to its value and makes enough money from the sale of each one to buy a new one and have another project while he and his family have a place to live. He says, "We certainly couldn't afford the house we live in now if we had not done some serious sweat equity work in Cleveland. Our current house is another fixer-upper, extending our housing dollars." While Chapa renovates, he says, "I do my own housework. No, not cleaning. I mean construction. Major construction. I am the original 'on-home' dad. The financial savings of doing my own construction work on our fixer-upper is approaching six figures, after six years."

Don't be afraid to ask questions, whether from a contractor giving you an estimate to a salesperson at a home improvement store. Once you get past any personal issues about asking another person for help, you'll find the financial savings worth it. And the satisfaction you get from completing a job—and doing it well— well, that's priceless. I've listed a few helpful home repair books and resources in the back of the book.

Shopping for Bargains

I have found that you can find some great bargains during the holiday sales or if you can catch a store that needs to get rid of excess

Do It Yourself With Your Kids

Looking for coupons in the papers is not only a great way to save money, it is also a task that you can share with your kids. Make it a race with your kids: whoever cuts the most coupons in an hour wins a prize, or whoever's coupons result in the biggest savings is the winner. Kids love to help out and will appreciate doing something that helps the family, too.

—From the Author

inventory. Once, at a local CVS, they had an oversupply of no-name dishwashing detergent. They were selling it for eighteen cents a bottle or $1.98 for a case of twelve. I figured this was my chance to load up in bulk. Imagine the shock of the salesperson when I ordered up twelve cases of the stuff. I got a kick out my wife's reaction when I drove in the driveway with a carload of dish detergent. I took the twelve cases and stuck it in the basement. It lasted about seven years. Since this first experience, when I see huge bargains, I load up.

Mike Donahue uses creative shopping and cooking to save.

We try to save money (I'm getting a little better) by using coupons, and by shopping at Super Wal-Mart. We only buy a limited supply of pop (or soda, depending on where you're from). And when it's gone . . . it's gone. The kids used to drink it all in two days and they all claimed to have had "only one." We eat a lot of potatoes and good bread with meals, along with a good protein source. I do most of the cooking during the week; we try to make meals that will last a few days, or more than one meal. We make our own potato chips and tortilla chips. I work in eggs a lot. We do Hamburger Helper—and yes, we do buy the family pack of frozen burgers—and we try to jazz it up with fresh veggies and spices. We try to work in homemade desserts and other fun foods . . . we bake.

Mike has done a great job here of being creative in his cooking and keeping the expenses down at the same time.

Potentially expensive food habits are good to break when the kids are young. When my first child, John, was born, I bought and fed him apple juice by the gallon. He was addicted to it. My sister mentioned that her kids drank water only, so I made the decision to stop any juice altogether and switch to water. My son was three at the time, and I told him that after the last bottle of apple juice, it was only water from then on. I then used a few Poland Spring bottles and kept them filled in the refrigerator at all times, and John got used to grabbing the water whenever he was thirsty. This alone saved $200–300 per year. Once John became used to drinking water and apple juice wasn't around, he didn't even ask for it after a few weeks. Using water also saved at McDonald's or the movies, since I wouldn't have to pay the high cost of the drinks and just brought a few bottles of water instead. Although most fast food restaurants don't charge for water (unless it's bottled), the kids do not automatically order a soda since they already have their drinks in hand. This move also may save on your dentist bill as well!

I hope this chapter has given you a few ideas on saving money. Basically, by changing your thinking on what you and your kids want as opposed to what you really need, you can easily downsize your lifestyle. Over time you will grow comfortable with this new financial routine. Remember, when you don't need money, you don't have the stress of having to make that extra money, and less stress means a happier family all around. In the next chapter, I will examine how some at-home dads supplement their incomes by working at home.

SPOTLIGHT ON DAD
"Trading Money for Love"

BY **WILLIAM DOLAN** *William Dolan resides in Liverpool, New York, with his wife and two daughters.*

It was never supposed to be this way. I was, after all, a trained professional. With my master's degree in environmental science in hand, I was sharing my wealth of knowledge and talents with the business world. Not one of those deplorable yuppies, mind you, just a young man fortunate enough to have actually found a job related to his education. I was on my way.

Raising children? Like most men, I'd heard of such a concept and never considered for even one brief moment that it might be something in which I would be heavily involved. My wife, I safely assumed, would be the primary care provider, while I would take my place as her humble assistant. She had always been wonderful with children. I would have no problem following her instructions. Hey, I was even willing to change a diaper once in a while.

Then a strange thing happened. When our first child was six months old, I was suddenly laid off from my job. My wife, also a professional, had only been back to work for about a month when I received the bad news. She had been on an extended maternity leave, and we were barely beginning to adapt to a hectic and complex life as two working parents. Now what were we going to do? No problem, I thought. I'll just find another job. Our daughter could stay in daycare while I informed corporate America of my availability. Since I wasn't working, I was in charge of transporting our daughter, Nicole, to and from daycare. That meant getting her dressed in the morning, feeding her, and packing her bag for the day. Outwardly simple tasks—which I found terrifying.

Despite my fears, I was able to get Nicole to the daycare center every day, sometimes even with her shoes on the right feet. And I would always pick her up at the last possible minute. She was, after all, in the hands of trained experts. The least I could do was allow them to give my daughter the care she deserved. I rejoiced in my own unselfishness. Then my wife had an idea. My job search had been progressing very slowly, and there was no reason why I couldn't spend an occasional day with Nicole. Just my daughter and me getting to know each other better. Childcare was expensive, and while we were not in a financial crisis, we could save a few dollars by using daycare three days a week instead of five. Neither my wife nor I had ever been crazy about putting our children in daycare anyway, so the idea seemed to make perfect sense. The only problem was that I always figured it would be my wife who stayed home. She always wanted to raise children, and we had discussed the possibility of her taking a leave of absence from her job. A great theory, with one major flaw: she had always made more money than I did.

Also, I had never been in charge of a small person who wore diapers and was incapable of holding an intelligible conversation. Despite my apprehension, Nicole started going to daycare three times a week. On Tuesdays and Thursdays she was all mine. The first few sessions are a bit hazy in my memory, possibly due to hysterical blackouts, but I'm certain those days consisted of little more than watching the clock to see how long it was until naptime. I muddled through the days she stayed home with me and looked forward to her next visit to daycare. While my job search continued to be unsuccessful, an old dream began to reappear in my head. I had always wanted to be a writer, ever since I was a little kid. I had even written a novel when I was in college, for no other reason than to see if I could. But for a million reasons I always kept the dream at bay. Too risky, not enough time, no financial security, and so on. Now, however, I was suddenly presented with the opportunity to give it a real shot. I discussed it with my wife, who offered only encouragement. "Go for it," she would tell me with conviction. Most people never get the chance to chase a dream. I could stay home with Nicole and write. Wait a minute here. Stay home with Nicole? And write? Was she serious? How could I possibly find the time to write, when the best I could do was finish each day a little bit behind where I was when it began? Writers need silence, they need solitude, and they need time for introspection. What I needed, I now realize, was a lesson, one that was finally taught to me by my daughter. Somewhere in the middle of all this chaos, I fell madly in love with Nicole. Trips to daycare were becoming less and less frequent, and I actually found myself taking her with me to visit friends and anywhere else I needed to go. She was my companion. I got a kick out of the goofy things she would do, and I marveled at the speed of her development and her voracious appetite for learning. I was happier now. Nicole was just as new at being a person as I was at being a parent. She never complained once.

I've been at this for more than three years now, as hard as that is to believe. Nicole is now a typical, happy-go-lucky four-year-old. She has the uncanny ability to completely frustrate me one minute, then make me laugh the next, which is not so unusual for someone not yet in kindergarten. And she also has a little sister, Brianna, a strong-willed type who currently seems set on remodeling our house. I make fewer mistakes now, and my wife, my harshest critic and strongest supporter, seems to think I'm doing a good job with them. I hope she's right.

The writing career continues to develop slowly, and I still have to put up with the funny looks, the supposedly funny comments, and the same tired questions. And as hard as I try not to, I wonder what people think. Do they respect me for what I'm doing, or do they think I'm wasting my time? Sometimes, usually during one of my bad days, I'll even ask those questions myself. I have a lot of education and work experience. Have I hung myself by staying out of the workforce for so long a period? Shouldn't I be making a pile of money somewhere, climbing the corporate ladder and keeping up with my neighbors? The rewards of raising children are never monetary, nor are they always clear or immediate.

I guess these are the questions all professional parents ask themselves. I like that term, by the way: *professional parent*. It's not perfect, but it beats *stay-at-home father*, and ranks way above *househusband*. All I'm asking for is a little respect. I deserve it. And if you call me Mr. Mom, I'll hit you with my diaper bag.

6

Working at Home: A Juggling Act

After a few months of being at home taking care of my first son, I realized that I had a little extra time on my hands. Since he was taking two naps each day at three hours apiece, I began thinking about how I could make some money at home without it getting in the way of my primary job: taking care of my son. Since my background involved journalism, photography, and computer programming, I came up with the idea of putting together a newsletter for at-home dads. It was the perfect job for me because I could apply my past experiences and skills, but I could also drop whatever I was doing when John needed me. Since I could interview dads and write my stories when my son was sleeping, I thought this was the perfect kid-friendly, at-home business. For other dads, however, the decision may not be so easy.

In this chapter I will look at the pros and cons of working at home and help you decide if you are a candidate for running a business out of your home with the kids around. If you are, I will show how to create the right job for you. I will give some examples of dads who are able to keep their work and home life separate without excluding the kids. I will also show you how today's technology can help make your home life stress-free.

Weighing the Pros and Cons

Before you begin daydreaming about what kinds of jobs you can do at home, make sure that the decision to work at home is right for you and your family. Do not let the motivation behind your decision be the male stereotypes that make you feel like you should be working for pay (as opposed to nonpaid work, such as raising your children) to support your family. First, write a list of pros and cons in terms of how working from home will affect you and your day-to-day life, and then ask the same questions while thinking of how this choice will affect your wife. Finally, make a list to detail the impact on your kids. Share these lists with your wife and discuss the issue. She might have some issues you haven't thought of or have an idea how to turn a con into a pro or vice versa. Making these kinds of lists will give you an idea of how working at home will affect the entire family before you commit to a side career.

These lists and exercises will help you determine what is realistic and what is not when considering starting (or buying) a home-based business. Now it's time to make one more list—this is the daily reality check. Sit down and write out an hour-by-hour schedule of your day. This will indicate when you could have time to work at home.

Often, dads who decide to work at home think they will have fewer demands on them at home than at the office, when in fact the opposite is true. Even when your kids are in school part of the day or nap for several hours at a time, working at home can be double duty. Jay Massey of Pensacola, Florida, an at-home dad working as a Web designer and the owner of www.slowlane.com, an online resource for at-home dads, describes a typical day:

> I have attended a Valentine's party at my son's preschool, had two meetings at clients' offices, lost a large contract that we bid on, played toddler street hockey, closed a deal by phone with another client on the other side of the country, cooked

dinner, watched the winter Olympics with my family, attempted an Internet conference, and now, in less than five hours, my son will be waking up ready for a new day.

Massey emphasizes that making the decision to work at home and be a full-time caregiver should not be taken lightly. "When you work at home you are, in effect, taking on a second job," Massey says. "Your family—the same family you decided to stay home and raise, the family that counts on you to be there—is your number one job. Anything else is secondary." Massey describes how dads need to really think through whether they can handle a second job and whether it is worth it, particularly because it will be another source of anxiety between a husband and wife. "Joann works a four-day work week and takes Tucker off my hands Friday, Saturday, and Sunday. I work during naptime, nights, and weekends. Staying and working at home is a positive for Tucker, but it is hard on Joann's and my relationship." His wife, Joann, gives this description of her life: "You know that feeling you have the night before you take a big trip? Running around all over the place trying to get everything? That's what it's like." Clearly, being able to multitask is an essential skill for at-home dads who are considering starting an at-home business.

Choosing the Right Job

In your search for a home business, probe your past jobs, hobbies, and old contacts to come up with ideas. If you have been in the same job for several years, it may be hard to figure out what other lines of work would best suit your talents. Create a list of things you wanted to be when you were a kid. Did you want to be a fireman? Maybe there is some way to be a volunteer in your town or to help out in other ways. Did you want to play football? Check out the local schools and see if they need another coach. Write down what clubs and sports you did in school as well as what hobbies you do now. Then think about the people with whom you come in contact in your life today. Does someone have a job that you always thought you wanted to do? Include that on the list, too. Start by dreaming big—without boundaries—and then go through the list and think about how you can make each option a real possibility. Not every item on this list will convert to a real possibility in reality—for instance, being the next Harrison Ford may not be an option—but at least this gets you into the mode of thinking outside the box. For each of the more realistic options, come up with

Computer Recycling

If you have updated your computer in the workplace, you probably have a stored, obsolete, or broken computer and keyboard lying around the basement. Here's a great way to recycle them and give your kids hours of doing what they like best: destroying. You just need the following:

    an old computer or the keyboard (don't include the monitor)
    Elmer's glue (or Tacky Glue)
    mat board or cardboard
    Phillips and flat-edge screwdrivers

Now put your computer piece in front of your kids and let them take it apart; they are genetically wired to do this, so no instructions are required. With all the stuff they pull out (keyboard letters, springs, wires, chips, and more), they can make a design on the cardboard by gluing the pieces on. This makes a great two- to three-hour project. You can try this at your own discretion, depending on the age of your child, with other small appliances. My kids loved this. Just don't forget to tell them to leave your current computer alone! Recommended for kids age five and older.

—From the Author

ways you can achieve those goals. Then revisit the list after a few days and see which ones you are the most excited about pursuing.

Upon learning that his wife was pregnant, one dad decided to resign as a computer specialist, and started giving piano lessons in his home after his wife returned from work. Within weeks, he had a few students taking piano lessons, and as word of mouth spread, he ended up opening a music studio. He says,

> In talking with a former colleague of mine, I found out tutoring makes good money, too. So I opened the business up to elementary tutoring. I made up some brochures and delivered half a stack to each of the ten or so surrounding elementary schools. I started receiving phone calls the next day! With a total of twelve students now, I am working Monday through Thursday evenings. There is pretty much a need for this type of service wherever there are kids, and the going rate around here is $35 to $40 an hour for music lessons. One part of my business that my children really enjoy is "Preschool Music Day Camp," held once a week for an hour during the day.

Of course, his son has become one of his students.

Peter Siler of Herndon, Virginia, is another dad who has made good use of his past skills.

> I always wanted to own my own business, so I decided to take advantage of my computer technology skills and become a home and small business computer consultant. I hung out my shingle, and through word of mouth mostly, I began to build the business. I found that, in general, there is a real need for computer help out there. The computer superstores of the world are just not helping people the way they want to be helped. This creates a strong market niche for those of us who are computer-savvy and like to help others.

In the above example, Siler was able to identify a need and fill it. He was also able to grow his business at a slow pace by using word of mouth instead of advertising. This way he can try a few small jobs to see how it affects his home life. If he can handle a few clients, then he can chose to increase his business a little or to keep it the way it is, depending on his workload.

Some dads I've spoken with turn to their kids for guidance on what kind of job they could do at home. What does a five-year-old know about making major life decisions? For those dads who have recognized the joy of being with their children at home, finding a career that can include spending time with them is incredibly rewarding. The wonderful thing I found in interviewing dads is how they are able to get their kids to enjoy and even get involved with the home-based business.

Take the unusual idea of Phil Isis of Greeley, Colorado, father of two boys in elementary school. He ran a business that every kid wished his dad would do: he became the ice cream man! Using a bicycle trailer that he built and one half of a large plastic portable doghouse, he would ride around stocked with ice cream sandwiches, Klondike bars, Eskimo Pies, low-fat yogurt bars, Italian ices, and frozen Snickers ice cream bars. With his two boys riding behind him on their bikes, he would sell his cold treats during hot summer days in Colorado. They ended up calling the venture Dog House Ice Cream. His biggest concern was that having his kids so close to the products would eat into the profits. But instead of eating their profits, they ended up selling to their friends. "We got great exercise, had lots of fun, and got to meet hundreds of car salespersons, real estate agents, and about any businessperson you can imagine. When you can take the summer heat and turn it into a positive growth opportunity for you and your kids, you're at the undergraduate level of the at-home universe." Of course, make sure you check with your city/town hall to see what is required from the board of health and what type of permit and liability insurance you will need for such an endeavor.

By including your kids in your work, you will be able to share some quality time and new experiences together. By having a kid-friendly business you can also teach them a sense of self-worth. For example, when Jack Cleary of York, Maine, started his search for a kid-friendly business, he was caring for his three-year-old daughter, Katie. What stood out in his mind was his daughter's love for animals. When they moved away from their New Jersey neighborhood and the pets she helped him care for, she cried because she missed the animals so much. With this in mind, he started a pet-sitting business called Petpals, one in which he could include Katie in his work. Cleary got his initial contacts by placing a small ad in the local shopping news, which brought him business almost immediately. Word of mouth helped him get two dogs to care for over the holidays. Over time he gained more clients, and before he knew it, Cleary and his daughter were walking and grooming dogs, too. Cleary says of his daughter, "She likes the variety that her involvement will bring. She has developed a respect for the job so when she does get a dog of her own, she will give the dog the care it needs. Also, she will not be wondering where her dad is because she will be helping with the grooming and walking." His daughter wants to be a veterinarian (for now).

In another example of following a child's passion, David Alpert of New York City started a video business that caters to the interests of kids. This business was inspired by his son, Luke. When he noted his son's fascination with construction sites, he decided to put together a video about a child who gets to explore a skyscraper while it's being built; the video features and explains how large construction equipment is used.

Alpert says, "I owe it all to Luke; if he hadn't been so fascinated with tower cranes and excavators, the idea would never have occurred to me." Alpert and his wife, Quincy, produced the video, and he also received outside help from an educator with video experience. The video, called *Building Skyscrapers*, has already won two children's video awards.

If you choose a job in which you can involve your children, then you don't have to make as many tough choices with your time, and you can still keep your primary role in mind while making some extra income.

Setting Reasonable Expectations

This brings me to the key to being able to work at home: setting reasonable expectations. Just as with housecleaning or cooking, make sure you understand what your expectations are for yourself and what others expect of you. Write out what you hope to achieve in running a business at home, and how you plan to achieve these goals. Speak to your wife about what she expects. Discuss the issue thoroughly and thoughtfully, using good communication techniques to realistically assess whether you can take on a second job, one that will always come second to your primary job of raising your children.

If you have young infants or preschoolers who need constant care, or if you have a job that requires constant use of the phone or meeting with clients at home, this will create an environment in which the kids are not involved in your work. In these cases, prepare yourself to work late hours when you might not be at your best, instead of early in the morning. If you don't like the idea of

Corrugated Highways

Here's a way to put those empty cardboard boxes that are lying around your home office to use. Open up both ends, slit one side, and you have a long piece on which to draw. Draw elaborate roadmaps, complete with railroad tracks, houses, fire stations, and more. When done, my son dumped his trillion little cars and made a "traffic jam." Great for all kids ages two and up.

—Holly Baylies, Stoneham, Massachusetts

working late into the night, you may want to choose other jobs that permit you to work while your kids are awake or napping. One dad describes how this sometimes works out for him: "Many times I have a deadline that forces me to work longer hours. The only hours available are those like right now—after midnight. It does not matter what time you go to bed, your child still wakes up at the same time. So working at home has had a serious impact on my sleep schedule."

In summary, visualize how your day will go if you run a particular business out of your home. If you do not have a kid-friendly business, then the kids cannot be in the same room with you or cannot help out. In this case, you'll need to be able to do this job after hours (such as after the kids are in bed for the night). If this doesn't sound like a workable solution for you, rethink your choice.

Daycare Dads

I have found an increasingly rapid blip on my fatherhood radar: at-home dads who run daycare centers, the ultimate kid-friendly business, out of their family homes. My first daycare dad sighting occurred in 1995, when I interviewed Peter Horn of Wauwatosa, Wisconsin. "Even before we were married," says his wife, Lynn, "we decided we wanted to raise our own children. This was very important to us." Since she had the better job as a claims examiner and he had the better patience, Peter gave up his construction truck-driving job to stay home with his newborn daughter, Casey. Needing extra income, they started thinking of home-based business ideas. They were determined not to be a split-shift family. The answer came when Lynn noticed how kids seemed to naturally be drawn to Peter. Seeing how much fun he seemed to have with children, she asked, "Why don't you do daycare?" Without flinching he said, "Yeah, I could do that."

After getting certified by the state agency and generally being run through the mill with background checks, home and health safety checks, and referrals, Horn put out an ad for his new business, called the Little Village Family Daycare. Right off the bat, he met one of the major hurdles that many daycare dads confront. His first call was from a father who, upon finding out the person staying home and running the daycare was a man, said "No way in hell I'd have a man with my boy." Undaunted, Horn ended up getting three toddlers by word of mouth through friends who knew he was great with kids, and he has now been running his daycare for three years.

When Eric, Danny, and Jazmyn come in each morning, Horn says he treats them just like an extended family. "We even have the parents over to relax out on the patio . . . better to do business with people who are my friends." Each day he makes breakfast as the kids come in around 7:30 to 8 A.M. Then it's a little Barney or cartoons as he cleans up. Weather permitting, he heads outside for some playtime. His outdoor activities range from chalk drawings on the sidewalk to field trips. As for the business end, he charges the going rate for each child based on his local area, which keeps the finances in order.

One dad who has received quite a bit of publicity is Dave Maxson of Westminster, Colorado, who runs Davey Bear's Daycare. He notes that in the beginning, seven out of ten callers would ask him for the person running the place, and when he responded, "You're talking to him," the next sound he would hear would be click—another hang-up. Now, he says, he gets only "three out of ten who hang up immediately." His most troublesome kid? "My daughter is the worst child I have. She gets the most time outs." John Wise of Portland, Maine, wanted to make it clear that a dad was running his daycare, so he named it Dad's Home Childcare. The first six months of his business were slow. His first client was someone no one else wanted, a special needs child with cerebral palsy. After some advertising, workshops, and networking, he found that word of mouth was what worked best. He now has eight kids in his care (two of them his own).

Chris Grimes of Des Moines, Iowa, took up the daycare business after six years working in a soybean factory. While he was working outside the home, his daughter went through two daycare situations that were unsavory. Soon he found himself taking childcare classes at a local college, and found that he "really liked being a parent" and wanted more time with his daughter. The only way he could do this and make money was to open his Tiny Days Daycare Center. Now in his third year of business, he has six clients, including his 3½-year-old daughter. He's had the same kids since he opened three years ago.

One interesting trend among the daycare dads was their insistence that there be little structure; they let the kids dictate their playtime. "It's art time around here if Joe says, 'Let's do art,'" says Wise. "The only structure around here is snacktime, naptime, and lunchtime." Wise calls it the rhythm method and explains it with, "Why would you want to break that rhythm by forcing another activity when everything is fine? If things are running smoothly, we will continue with it as long as the kids are enjoying it." Horn agrees. "If one of my kids finds a bug on the sidewalk and wants to talk about bugs, I take it as far as he wants it to go. I call it a teachable moment, when their interest is at a peak." Jim Marzano of Kingston, New York, who runs what he calls "artcare," charges more than a standard daycare since he cares for his kids in his art studio. He says, "In my art studio, kids rule. I have no predetermined schedule. Each day they come in and I pick their brains."

While there are more dads taking on the daycare role, it's not a job that you can assume lightly. Beyond all the paperwork and training you need to go through to be certified to run a daycare center, the day-to-day job can be exhausting. But if you think you can do the job, you need to consider a few things, such as:

- Is there a need for daycare in your area?
- What age children should you accept? Infants? Toddlers?

- Do your home and backyard comply with your state's standards for daycare centers?
- Will you need to make any renovations to your home?
- What type of licenses and permits will you need?
- What should you charge for your services?
- What type of equipment and toys will you need?
- What activities will you use with the kids in your care?

See the resource section in the back for recommended books that will expand on the list above on running a daycare center.

Getting to Work

Once you have laid the groundwork for what your new position will entail, you need to figure out how to work both jobs and be good at both—no small feat! While I had it easy, since most of the people I spoke to for my job were other at-home dads and were thus very understanding when they heard a child screaming in the background, most dads are not this lucky. It is important to have a

---

The Sunday Paper

Ah, Sunday morning! The paper is ready for you at the door—but how to get quiet time so you can read the paper with the kids? First, for the two- to three-year-olds, get the coupon section and cut the pictures out for your kids. Then get out the glue and construction paper to keep them busy and happy while you read the sports and funnies or your favorite section. For kids four and older, just toss them the coupons and scissors and see what they can come up with. When you are done with the funnies, pass them on to the kids for destruction.

—*From the Author*

---

set of tricks on hand to deal with emergency situations, such as when a client needs to speak to you and your child is throwing a temper tantrum. If you have the luxury of being able to take on responsibilities slowly, it will help you juggle your two roles.

Here are a few helpful tips to manage your time and make your double-duty lifestyle as easy as possible:

1. **Turn to technology.** Since kids can be unpredictable, making use of telecommunications advancements can help. One dad found that by using a feature that assigns different rings for business calls (two short rings) than for personal calls (regular rings), he is able to distinguish a call from wherever he is in the house, no matter what he's doing, and decide if he should take the call at that moment.

> If a business call rings and my son is yelling for Jell-O, I don't pick up the phone. I let the answering machine get it. . . . You might think caller ID already accomplishes identifying the call, but I still like the feature of different rings. Sometimes I don't want to run through the family room and into the kitchen to check the caller ID. The special ring instantly tells me the type of call, without having to interrupt playtime with the kids.

Also, some inexpensive headsets include a mute button, so if you're on a business call and your child starts the siren cry for help, then you can keep your client from hearing this and, when possible, tell the client you'll need to call him/her back.

Jay Massey agrees that using technology has helped him better manage his time.

> With my son starting school, I went from stay-at-home dad to work-at-home dad. At that time, my pager was replaced by a cell phone, not as much to be available for calls, but as a time management tool. Tucker is in school six hours during

the day, and that's when I focus on business. But if I am away from my home office running errands or meeting with clients, I found that when I would get back I would have a pile of calls to return. These phone calls sometimes cut into daddy–son time if there were more than a few important ones. Now, with the cell phone, I can check my voice mail on the way in (yes, I use a headset so I can drive safely with both hands) and start returning the important calls right away. For me, technology (computer, Palm Pilot, cell, pager, and so on), when used prudently, improves my ability to balance home, family, work, and Slowlane.com, so it's not more hurried.

If you are tech-savvy, these solutions might also work for you.

2. **Plan "quick quiet breaks" for your kids.** You are playing with your son and suddenly the phone rings. You answer it, and while you are talking business on the phone, your child goes nuts and screams for your attention. How many times has this happened to you? Not only is your child screaming, but the caller may think twice before visiting your home. Of course, you can let the call go to your answering machine and call back during naptime. However, there will be times when you have to make or receive calls to get some information now. If you plan ahead for "quick quiet breaks," you can avoid this panic time and maybe save a customer. Here are three things you can do in an emergency:

- Always have a favorite juice or snack ready.
- If your children have a favorite video, have it ready to pop in the VCR.
- If all else fails, and you must stay on the phone, have a stash of new toys your children have never seen and give them one. This will almost always stop them in their tracks as they excitedly play with the new toy.

3. **Establish your workspace as a no-play zone.** Working at-home dads agree that making it clear to kids that the office is not a play space is essential not only to your professional life, but also to your sanity. One father from Commack, New York, describes an instance when his four-year-old son learned how to delete files.

> I put about forty hours into this particular project. I walked into the studio one day to set up for my clients' return that evening, to find my Mac on. . . . The screen saver was activated and my son was sitting in a play area, so I deactivated the screen saver to see hundreds of windows opened on my desktop. I started closing all the windows and looking for the files I needed to prepare for the night's session. I searched frantically and could not find anything on the hard drive. I freaked out because I didn't back the files up.

While he was able to retrieve his files using data recovery software, his lesson was learned: don't underestimate what damage can be done, no matter how small or young the child.

If You Can't Lick 'Em

Last December, Caitlin (almost three at the time) and I came up with a fun way for her to help with the Christmas card envelopes. We used a paintbrush from her water-painting books to dampen all the envelope flaps. Each dip in the water provided just the right amount of moisture to seal one flap. She had fun painting the envelopes and I didn't have to lick all that glue or risk a very painful paper cut on the tongue.

—*Scott Hahn, Richmond, Virginia*

4. **Keep work and home separate.** This is sometimes the most difficult challenge for working-at-home dads, and the most important to learn. If for no other reason, it is important to separate work from home to make sure that even though you may have been jumping from dad mode to work mode all day, you are able to walk away from the "office" when it is time to be with the family. Whether this means creating a completely separate space for your office work, or just allotting certain hours for it, it is essential that there is a point where you leave your office and return home. One dad, who works as an architect at home, said starting a routine as if he were going to the office was key to keeping the two realms separate. He went as far as creating a separate door to his office so that he could literally step outside his front door and enter his office. "I have found that having a separate entrance to the office makes me feel like I'm going to work instead of just going to the basement. Also shower, shave, and look like you're going to work. It will change your outlook a lot."

5. **Don't shut out your children.** This may seem to contradict numbers 2 and 3 above, but while you want to set your office space up as a place of business and make that clear to the children, you also want to take advantage of one of the best parts of working at home: you can still spend time with the kids during the day, and they can learn all about another side of you that they would normally not be able to see. Richard Louv, from San Diego, California, a freelance journalist and stay-at-home dad, describes some of these perks:

> Working from home offers immeasurable fringe benefits. The comfort of proximity and time. The Post-it love notes from the grade-schooler. The self-portraits stuck to my computer screen. My knowledge that they are safe. The overheard conversations between the brothers, the sudden revelations about their lives.

Louv goes on to point out that all of the benefits are not only appreciated by him, but also by his children.

> To Matthew and Jason, the adult work world is not some mysterious and closed box, but a familiar doorway, an opportunity. They learn by osmosis as they overhear my phone interviews. They know my work personality. They understand that I sometimes feel frustrated and even defeated by work, but never permanently.

So invite your kids in and let them learn from you just like you are constantly learning from them.

6. **Keep your home business home.** Finally, before you take the plunge in starting your business, don't forget a very important aspect that could make you bankrupt overnight: your neighbors. If your business needs just a computer, modem, and a phone (such as mine), then read no further, no one will be the wiser. Make sure whatever you decide to do, you keep a low profile. If you have clients that frequently drop by and tie up parking, it can upset your neighbors, who may complain to the police. The solution: try to keep visits to a minimum by conducting business over the phone or e-mail, if you have it. If your kids can play by themselves, take them to the local playground and meet your client there. While your kids are happy playing, you have a relaxed, stress-free atmosphere to talk business, while still keeping an eye on your kids. On the other hand, if you choose to run a home-based airport limo service business and you become too successful, your nice next-door neighbor may not be too happy with your three vans lined up on the street. Then it's time to rent some commercial space away from your neighbors.

SPOTLIGHT ON DAD
Seven Home-Based Businesses

I'd like to end this chapter with seven stories about at-home dads who have successfully run kid-friendly businesses. I present these stories because all the dads featured below meet two important criteria in starting a business. First, the cost of start-up is low. Most important, they love what they do. These are dads who simply decided to "follow their bliss," as renowned professor of mythology Joseph Campbell puts it. This is essential if you are going to be raising your kids at the same time—it's easy for kids to pick up on whether a parent is happy or not. As you read these stories, you may find one that matches your interests, current area of expertise, what you aspire to achieve, and/or find tips to help you improve the choices you've already made. I hope these stories inspire you.

"At-Home Disc Jockey Daddy," a profile of Gerry Bradshaw

BY PETER BAYLIES *Gerry Bradshaw is from Fredericksburg, Virginia.*

It was a disc jockey's worst nightmare—while spinning CDs at a wedding, the groom's father had a heart attack and was carried right off the dance floor into an ambulance. This would have ended most weddings, but Gerry Bradshaw took a chance. "I grabbed the microphone after fifteen minutes and announced that he was going to be fine," he remembers. Gerry's quick thinking saved the party, and it went on for another three hours. (Turns out the father actually was OK.)

These days Bradshaw, an at-home dad during the week, changes into his tux every weekend to attend yet another wedding or to start another party where he works as a DJ. He has four boys ages ten, thirteen, fifteen, and twenty-five. His love of music dates back to his teenage years, and he went to the FCC at twenty-four years old to get his radio disk jockey license. In the early 1980s, his first marriage ended, and he started attending the singles clubs sponsored by Parents Without Partners. "They had dances on Friday nights with a lousy disc jockey who was getting $50 a night. Being divorced, I needed the money, so I grabbed the job," he says. Soon the single folks he knew at these functions started getting married and began hiring him to do their weddings. In 1987, Bradshaw married a woman he met DJing one night. The next year Patty and Gerry had their first child. Since Patty was working the weekly nine-to-five shift for the federal government as a Defense Department investigator, there was no discussion on who would stay home with the kids.

When Patty was transferred from her Miami branch in 1990, Gerry followed her career just south of Washington, D.C., to Fredericksburg, Virginia, where he had to build his reputation from scratch. At this time, the youngest baby was under a year old and two others were preschool age. "All you need to start up this business is a natural love for music and high-quality stereo equipment," says Bradshaw. Of course, using your personal, average-quality equipment should be limited to the backyard picnics, schools, and VFW functions. For larger venues you need to start with about $2,000. You may need to upgrade to a pro line of speakers and amps that can be found at guitar and drum stores. Bradshaw even uses special effects, such as multicolored lighting that changes with the music, and that you can buy for around $200.

Bradshaw checks out other DJs from time to time to see what they do. "One day I was listening to a DJ at a party and he was lousy, so bad he even played the same song in the space of three hours," Bradshaw says. The fellow DJ approached Bradshaw after his gig and compared his pricing. When he discovered that this DJ charged $300, Bradshaw upped his own price to $500 from $400. In August of 2002, he raised his fee to $1,000 for weddings, and he gets it due to the demand for his work. He's even done gigs for some celebrities, such as Billy Joel.

He says, "It's foolish to start off doing weddings. Start at the school parties and company picnics. This way you can get the feel for the small stuff." Bradshaw emphasizes, "You need the personality and the talent for being the life of the party. But at the same time be careful not to steal the limelight." Before you buy any equipment, check out the local DJs in the area and ask if they need any help.

Phone work is minimal during the week, around ten hours. Bradshaw's twenty-five-year-old son is now working as a DJ at a Vermont college and takes Bradshaw's ten-year-old out to do elementary parties together. Bradshaw, says, "It's a hoot, I pay him 10 percent. Once a client gave him a $50 tip and I split it with him. He made fifty-five bucks that day and was living large!"

"Teaching Kids Computers"

BY STEPHEN HOUSE *Stephen House is from Olympia, Washington.*

My son, who is 2½, really enjoys the time we spend together on our computer. I began working with him when he was 1½ after I noticed how interested he was in what I was doing on the computer. I was able to locate some age-appropriate and inexpensive shareware, and began spending a few minutes each day with him right before his nap. He loved it. After I had been an at-home dad for a few months, I started thinking about the possibilities of tutoring children as a business. *Entrepreneur* magazine identified a couple of franchises for computer kids and I called on one, but it had already been sold for this area. I began wondering how I could do this myself. During a one-day class on starting a business, I began exploring more ideas on how I could make this happen. Several of these ideas required a large initial investment and seemed a little too aggressive to start out.

After about six months of thinking about the idea, things started to come together. A lady who my wife works with wanted to know if I would tutor little kids (she has a nephew my son's age and had noticed how my son had progressed on his alphabet, colors, numbers, etc.). Another lady at my son's preschool with whom I had shared some kids' software was also interested in it for her daughter. Then, that same weekend, my sister-in-law mentioned that her daycare had a computer business come in to train groups of kids. The idea was starting to gel now.

My first phone call was to a daycare that my son had attended. They were very interested in my idea and wanted to see me. I spent the next three weeks getting things together, like buying some inexpensive PC hardware, loading it up with software, creating some hand-out materials, getting a business license, etc. Most of this work was done during my son's naptime (two to three hours) or late at night after everyone was asleep. I set up a date with the daycare, did my initial demo, and then waited for their call. They called back, and not only were they still interested in my tutoring program, but they hired me to conduct a couple of computer classes for their five-to-nine-year-olds during their summer program. They also said that they would watch my son while I was tutoring and try to give me a break on their hourly rates. Well, the daycare handed out an informational sheet on my business, and I'm scheduled to be there to display some programs and answer questions for any curious parents.

My current plans are to focus on one daycare for the moment, get the business kinks worked out, then, this fall, expand and offer the program to other daycare centers. Who knows? All it takes is an idea, a strong desire, and, of course, TIME.

"Going, Going . . . Gone!"

BY PHIL ISIS *Phil Isis lives in Greeley, Colorado.*

My story begins as the resident house dad in my neighborhood for the last five years. Despite numerous attempts to connect with some kind of home-based business, nothing seemed to work. I spent a lot of time doing home improvement projects to reassure myself that I was still a man, yet no matter what I managed to improve or accomplish, there was no substitute for good, old-fashioned money. (If you don't believe me, just ask my wife.) After much research, networking, and a master's degree, I discovered the antiques and collectibles business.

Buying and selling antiques, collectibles, or other items is certainly not unique. Many people make a very good living from this type of marketing. Just about everyone collects something; it's just a matter of what you can afford. I had been active in collecting with my kids for years, so it was only natural to take it to the next level. We've collected everything from baseball cards to coins and stamps, and this was a spontaneous jump to turn a hobby into a business. Getting started in the antiques and collectibles business was pure enjoyment for me. I went to the library and checked out several books on the topic, including auction how-to, collecting specialties, magazines, newsletters, and other reference sources. By the end of the first month, I had attended several auctions, covering everything from classics to junk. I was getting familiar with the rhythm of the auctioneers and the pulse of the buyers. I was starting to get the fever.

I've been involved in the buying and selling of antiques and collectibles for almost a year now. It has turned out to be an ideal home-based business and continues to grow and produce. The most rewarding aspect of the venture is that I am able to include my children in the business with me. As many of you already know, some home-based businesses can create as many problems as they solve. This occurs when you become torn between how much time to spend with the kids and your commitment to the needs of the business. I've listened to other dads who suffer tremendous guilt when they are unable to take their child to one soccer practice or attend some special event at school. This business has allowed convenient flexibility for my schedule, and the bulk of the auctions are held while my kids are in school.

I've been to multiple garage sales, estate sales, and flea markets and followed up on numerous classified ads. I've networked with a lot of folks who have been in the business. The whole family is excited about this business, and we all enjoy looking at and wondering about the old things that come into our house. I've already made plans to put on a couple of antique shows at the elementary school. There is nothing like sharing the knowledge of something you enjoy with the children.

The other side of this business is the selling part. There are as many ways to sell your antiques and collectibles as there are to buy them. Some of the choices are: auction consignments, booths at antique shows, antique malls, flea markets, consignment and antique shops, and classified ads in antique-trading newspapers. The reward of this venture is the joy of finding those rare bargains you got because everyone else was asleep, or being a hero in front of your kid because you managed to get—for an almost magical deal—that item they wanted. My wife has also gotten into the business. She has taken her old Barbies out of storage, and she swears the Beatles stuff is around here somewhere.

"Escape from Corporate America"

BY JOHN SLEVENS *John Slevens lives in Berkeley Heights, New Jersey. His Web site is www.unclejohnspuppets.com.*

It has been almost two years since I left the corporate world in pursuit of a dual career as an at-home dad and puppeteer. My new career direction was largely prompted by my three former employers, which relocated, merged, and went out of business. My last company required me to work out-of-state. After spending all of the summer and early fall away from my family, I finally said my farewells to my coworkers and embarked on a new dual career as a puppeteer and at-home father.

I had done puppet shows on occasional weekends more as a hobby than as a career. I did a lot of shows for free, especially for local hospitals. I chose puppetry, because I love making kids laugh, and I am plugged in as to what children in the three-to-five-year-old age group find funny. I knew that within a twenty-mile radius of where I live, there were many affluent towns where hiring an entertainer for a child's birthday party was very common. I had the gift to mimic character voices, and I was becoming very adept at puppetry.

Business is growing steadily, and I bring my sons (eight and twelve) along with me after school, on school holidays, or during the summer. They go in the box and bring up the puppets as I tell the audience (while I'm outside of the box) that the puppets aren't real and can't come up by themselves. I have been known to get big tips when my kids come along. As the months went by, I felt myself regaining all the confidence I lost over the years working in the corporate environment. I rekindled my close relationship with my sons and became more adept at running a home.

My supplies consist of the following: a puppet box that I built myself; two mini-spotlights; a gold shimmering curtain, which hypnotizes the kids when the colored spotlights are on it; a mini-cassette player; a 20 Watt Radio Shack PA with a microphone; and twenty-nine puppets, which run the gamut from a baby lion to an Indian princess to a power hero, in addition to my own "generic" puppets (which are Old McDonald, three monkeys, a skunk, an alligator, a shark, etc.). The start-up costs consist of the above items plus business cards and the price to advertise in a good, local children's magazine.

These publications are the best way to get the word out about your show. However, I'm competing with the traditional clowns, magicians, storytellers, and others. Word of mouth and people who saw me before and asked for my card continue to be 60 percent of my business. Repeat customers are 10 percent, and the kids' publications can range from 30 to 40 percent of initial business.

The shows I put on are usually for birthdays, but I can do theme parties, like "Reading Is Fun" or specials like Noah's Ark or Daniel in the Lion's Den. The only type of show I really do with any great frequency is a cross between stand-up comedy, singing kids' songs, telling corny kids' jokes, and creating the illusion of the puppets being chased by a wolf or a spider. I add current popular music with some 1950s songs rolled in, but the real trick is for the puppets to talk with the audience or kids during the show. My weekend schedule varies with a show or two on Saturday and the same on Sunday. My weekdays are filling up with schools, organizations, hospitals, churches, and more, as I get more popular.

The typical three-to-five-year-old will laugh just as hard at the same joke the twelfth time as he did the first time. Potty humor is big. The wrong words to songs are also a hoot! Finally, you have to be tuned into what three-to-five-year-olds are into. The resource for puppeteers is the Puppeteers of America. This is a group of professionals who put out newsletters, directories, and the like, of interest to professionals. There is a magazine called *Laugh-Makers*, which is for clowns, magicians, and puppeteers. They offer some tips on doing shows and more.

"Web Design"

BY HAL LEVY *Hal Levy lives in Manalapan, New Jersey. He's also reachable online at hlevy@daddyshome.com.*

When my daughter was born, I became an at-home parent. Before I started the most rewarding job of my life, I was working with a friend trying to build a consulting company. The company didn't work out, which turned out for the best, since I truly got to experience my daughter growing up. She is one of three children. I have two older sons aged eleven and twelve.

When I am not busy being a caregiver, I try to be an Internet consultant. For most of my clients, I develop Web systems. However, I also work with hardware and software related to the Internet. Internet consulting is not always the most profitable business to be in, and it is certainly a lot of work to keep up on the latest technology. It is no longer enough to know HTML (Hyper Text Markup Language). Now you need to know Java, Java Script, Perl, and SQL. You need to know VB Script, Active X, Visual Basic, Lingo, and C++. Every day there is more to learn. Before long we will need to have specialists. Static content is no longer acceptable. Web pages must now be dynamic and responsive to user interaction. Searchable databases and Macromedia games are the rage. We used to talk about interactive TV. Now it's the World Wide Web.

The cost of entry into Web development is low. If you have a computer, you have the basic tools already. You need a computer with some form of text editor (Notepad for Windows users is fine). There you go; you have all the tools you need to develop a basic Web site, albeit a static one. Now you need the knowledge. There are many Web sites that are devoted to instructions in HTML and Web development. You can't go into most bookstores without finding a plethora of Internet development books on the shelf. There are quite a few training options available. You can live at the local bookseller, purchase online- or CD-based training, or you can go for professional training. Professional training, however, can cost over $2,000, so be prepared for that expense! Of course, it can't hurt to be familiar with how to make quality images and animations. There is a whole other world of training in the graphic arts and using programs such as Paint Shop.

Once you have a basic education, start by making your own personal Web page. Be adventurous! Try to play with as much of the technology as you can. Make a great Web page advertising your work and start to find clients. Right now, the best market for new development is with small regional companies. Join your local Chamber of Commerce and try to entice the members to use your services through discounts or other motivators. After you establish your customer base, word of mouth from those customers to other small businesses is the best way to grow. Be sure you're familiar with all parts of the business! Have contacts so you can host the Web sites for your customers. Establish a repeat billing relationship. There are quite a few companies that are in business to host small Web sites. Most of these have reseller programs, so you can get paid monthly for hosting. Perhaps you would prefer to get paid a referral fee; some hosting companies do that also.

Because it isn't complex to become an Internet developer, there is quite a bit of competition. Always remember, you need to keep your priority, your family, firmly in front of you. Make sure you're doing this in time that you would otherwise spend watching television or sleeping. Trying to squeeze all of this between changing diapers, playing, and feeding isn't easy! Don't forget, dinner needs to be ready when your wife gets home from work! I have the advantage of having two preteen sons to help around the house. They do chores like putting the dishes in the dishwasher or taking out the garbage. But they also need care and attention! Time must be set aside for helping them with their homework, driving carpools, or just being there to listen. I have to get it all done. I need to be focused as a parent, make sure the projects get done, and keep up with the ever-changing technology. Not only do you have the standard responsibilities that the average at-home mother has, but you will also find you are still responsible for the garbage, repairing the car, and changing lightbulbs—tasks the average at-home mom would leave for Dad to do when he got home from his normal workday. Often you will find many things on your "to do" list undone. Don't let it get to you; move them to tomorrow's "to do" list and keep plugging along. Your kids are worth it.

I have had a number of annoying experiences since I took on the job title of "At-Home Parent." There was the eye doctor, who, in an effort to have a conversation with me, told me how he knew how it felt to be "stuck babysitting." Then there was the time at a local strip mall when a senior gentleman remarked, "Don't you hate it when they [wives] leave you to watch the baby?" I have had both women and men try to commiserate with me by telling me how unfair it was that my wife has burdened me with childcare. Pat yourself on the back, since everyone else is likely to question your decision. You're an at-home dad; you are doing the most important job in the world.

"Breakfast in Bed Every Day?"

BY WALT CHORLE   *Walt Chorle runs the Centennial Rose Bed & Breakfast in Philipsburg, Pennsylvania. You can visit him at www.centennialrose.com or reach him at (814) 342-4141.*

In addition to staying at home with my daughter, Sarah, I am operating our family-owned business, the Centennial Rose Bed & Breakfast. We bought the property in 1994 with a dual intention. My wife, Lisa, loves Victorian houses, and I have always been an entrepreneur, so I suggested pursuing the inn-keeping tradition. Expectations were low from the start, since originally this was a third job (we both worked full time pre-Sarah). We did not feel much risk. The business is definitely cyclical, so we started during the fall, which is peak season, and really never have been completely lacking for guests. We have stumbled into some good luck on occasions as well as had our challenges. This is not unlike any other type of business.

Since we live in the house that we periodically rent out, I must tell you that it is rather challenging to effectively watch Sarah and still maintain excellence in customer service. However, many guests are smitten with her, plus it may even enrich their visit, since our bed-and-breakfast treats a guest like a member of the extended family. Though it often is challenging logistically, my wife and I have steadily increased the bed-and-breakfast business while committing more time to Sarah. But before you can say "get rich quick," take a few points of caution before opening a bed-and-breakfast. Do not open one if any of these areas makes you squeamish: constant towel and bedding laundry, toilet duty, last to go to bed and first to get up (and being pleasant on both ends), cleaning up after a rowdy wedding party, and almost seeing two somewhat overweight, middle-aged honeymooners buck naked in your public hot tub at 7 A.M.!

The start-up expenses are heavy, and may include acquiring many antique furnishings, property improvement, nuisance local governmental assessments, and marketing. One major benefit is the tax write-off status of your home. A word of caution here is that bed-and-breakfasts do and will get audited, so if your heart is not in promoting and developing the business, expect a challenge. Renting several rooms a year may not give you the right to deduct a major portion of your house. See an accountant before submitting your first Schedule C.

I am lucky to be an entrepreneur and an active father. One thing all dads should realize is that you should not blindly accept that you must work out of the house and away from your child. Use your skills so that someday you will have a similar opportunity to what I have had. Money can't buy everything.

"Needed: Rubber Snakes and Chickens," a profile of Mike Bigman

BY PETER BAYLIES *Mike Bigman lives in Springfield, Virginia. His e-mail address is Biggo2@aol.com.*

Mike Bigman, a manager at a Ground Round restaurant, unknowingly started a new career thanks to a mistake by one of his employees. Turns out a hostess scheduled a birthday party on a day that the birthday clown wasn't working. When the customer complained, Bigman reassured her there would be a clown that day. He ended up putting on the clown outfit, complete with makeup and big shoes, and pulled off the act. "The kids liked me and I realized how easy it was, so I kept doing the clown act myself, since I had more parties scheduled in advance." After leaving that job, he took a ten-week clown class for $50. With that course he was able to incorporate what he learned as a clown with more visuals.

At first he used local advertising and worked for a few agents, but frustrated with their 30 to 40 percent charges, he did the legwork himself. He found the yellow pages got him a lot of calls. When he had his first son, Jared (now fourteen), it was tough adjusting, although the baby slept a lot. On one last-minute job, he brought the baby along, and Bigman reports, "As long as he had a bottle, he was OK." He says working on the phone when the kids are making noise is hard. He notes, "I want to give the impression that I have an office, but it's hard to do with my son yelling in the background, 'Dad, I need to go to bathroom.'" He was also able to hire a personal answering service for $60 a week, so he didn't have to worry about missing calls while he was out of the home.

Bigman has since had a second son, Reid, and he likes to involve both kids in his act. When he wants Reid to come along to guess the color of a napkin, he will whisper loud enough for all to hear, "Just say it's blue, and I will take you for ice cream." He notes, "When the kids started laughing the first time I did it, I saw something click in him, and he became part of the show. Later on at a party at a daycare, he saw me do two to three shows, so he really knew all the acts and he would finish off all the punch lines." His oldest son, Jared, is starting to get bored with the act. Bigman says, "Everyone is screaming and laughing, and he says, 'Oh no, not that one again.'"

The bulk of his business? "I do birthday parties mostly, restaurants like Fudruckers ($50 an hour), and I work every weekend three to four shows per day." Now he works as an agent to refer other clowns. He charges around 10 percent for his services. Bigman notes that 60 percent of his business is now word of mouth, 30 percent from the yellow pages, and 10 percent from local papers. Reflecting back, he says, "My mother used to do all her own parties, but now I deal with women vice presidents and lawyers with their power jobs. At the thought of having fifteen kids at their house, they say, 'Forget it!' They are terrified of it. I have to hold their hands. I tell them, 'You just need to serve cake and ice cream.'" While neither of Bigman's kids aspires to be a clown when they grow up, he notes that this isn't really the point. "They see what I do and that I enjoy it. They pick up on that."

Start-up costs are fairly minimal. Bigman paid the most money for his brochure, and he paid $1,500 for the initial artwork and printing. He owns two clown outfits at $200–300 each. A ten-week clown class costs $50 and clown makeup is $20; paying for magic trick secrets can cost $50–100. Other materials involve puppets, clown-type shoes, rubber snakes, rubber chickens, wands, a foam camera, and, of course, balloons to make those balloon animals. Learning to juggle helps, too. His favorite routine is playing music while juggling. "The music stops and starts again at random; I say I can't juggle when the music stops, and the kids love it. Getting kids to laugh is really easy, anything with repetition—they laugh harder the second or third time. When I juggle, I keep dropping the balls, and every time I pick them up, I drop another one, and they laugh even harder." He says this style of joke is hard on his wife. "But it's addictive to make people laugh and make them feel good; it gets in your blood. Many retired people do it just for fun. I kid her. She can't believe people would laugh at these things. I tell her I might get a real job when I grow up, but I'm trying to put it off as long as I can."

7

Avoiding At-Home Dad Burnout

Advice for the day: If you have a lot of tension and you get a headache, do what it says on the aspirin bottle: "Take two aspirin" and "Keep away from children."

—Author Unknown

My first few months with my newborn child were a breeze, since John slept several hours throughout the day. During waking hours, I enjoyed peaceful stroller walks and easy trips to the grocery store, where I was the center of everyone's attention with comments by women such as, "Oh, look at that father with his adorable baby." The night was tougher, but luckily my wife was willing to tend to most of his nighttime cries. I thought that if this was my new life, then it was going to be a cinch!

However, as the months passed, I found myself grabbing freeze pops for John so I could get five minutes of quiet, then sticking him in his Jolly Jumper to get ten minutes more. As John started walking, I could still buy some time with a Tootsie Roll lollipop, but with his mobility, the top of every table was in danger. Everywhere I looked, there was another Lego, Matchbox car, a half-eaten cracker, or a used baby wipe on the floor. Between the whining of the vacuum cleaner and the whining from my son, I was starting to lose it.

When my second son, David, was born (John was three at the time), there were more diapers to change, more dishes to clean, and even more crying (which I didn't think was possible). With two babies, I found myself running around to pick up after them, making sure they were safe, feeding and cleaning them, making dinner for my wife, and trying to run my other day-to-day errands. I distinctly remember the moment of no return—it was raining outside, the house was a mess, both babies were wailing, and I did not know what to do. We had watched all the videos in the house at least seventy times, and I couldn't bring myself to put on yet another *Rugrats* episode. I sat down on my couch and thought, "God, I need to get out of here." Trouble is, I had no time to reflect on it because I had to clean the pee behind the toilet before my wife got home.

In this chapter I will discuss the signs of burnout and give you some solutions to combat it. I will demonstrate how to get out of the house with the kids and to take time for yourself. In addition, I will explain how to deal with and avoid stress in your marriage, learn to control your anger, and come to take everything in stride.

Watching for the Signs

"Some dads suffer in silence," says Dr. Bruce Drobeck, a marriage and family therapist from Dallas.

> We may have more in common with at-home moms than the traditional working dad. The nontraditional lifestyle is a test of our marriage, and you really have to work together to make it work. At-home dads need individual time with the wife and time with the kids to balance out the new lifestyle.

When the children are young, you get the most stress at home, since they are totally dependent on you. As long as the youngest child doesn't know enough to stay off the road, your brain is always working at some level; it's never really at peace. The only way you can get more is to allow yourself to take a time out. Of course, with kids in tow and a diaper that needs to be changed at any time, you just can't. No matter how much you love them, you eventually need the time for yourself and begin to feel trapped and alone, which can be a warning sign of burnout.

Some of the signs of burnout include:

- Increasing feelings of impatience with your kids and the urge to shuttle them to the television or video games every time they come to you;
- Feelings of stress and resentment toward your wife;
- Lack of participation in your children's interests;
- Feeling the need to get out of the house alone;
- Missing the companionship of other adults or your former coworkers.

Setting up a plan to deal with burnout may be as important for your marriage as it is for your own well-being. Here are some solutions for you.

Sextuplet Tips

1. If they're happy, you're happy. When they're content, don't do anything to mess it up. Just sit back and enjoy the relative silence.
2. Don't rock the kids to sleep every night. If you rock them to sleep, then every time they wake up, including the middle of the night, they'll expect the same treatment. Trust me: you don't have that much free time.

—*Keith Dilly, Indianapolis, Indiana, father of sextuplets*

Getting Out

Burnout is inevitable, and it is important that you set up certain escapes for yourself to help deal with it in a safe and effective way. Again, it's important to be aware of how you are feeling and know when it's time to get out—whether it is for an hour or for a weekend. Sit down with your wife and create a plan that will allow you to get out of the house on a periodic basis. At least with a schedule, you can have something to look forward to when the days seem too overwhelming.

Sometimes when your spouse feels overwhelmed, this affects your quality of life, too. Alan Carroll of Brookline, New York, noted that his wife also suffers from burnout.

> My wife works a lot, and I think she is pulled between her work and her baby, so when she is at home she feels so guilty that she has to spend more time with the baby. As a result she neglects herself for the baby. She needs to take more time for herself.

He finds that his wife's refusal to take time for herself causes stress and arguments.

> When I say I want to go out and do something on my own, she will say, "Well, don't we have to buy a car seat," or something that might prevent me from taking time for myself. Then she will say, "But that's OK, go ahead." She plants that seed of guilt in my head that I am neglecting the baby. It's not like I am going to go to a strip club and pretend I am single. It's just that I know I need that time for myself. It gives me balance in my life, and I know that makes both me and the baby happy. The other day I was at a coffee shop with my daughter and I overheard two mothers talking. They were

saying that they need their personal time at the local gym so they could have the energy to give to the children. I wish my wife had heard that conversation.

Clearly, a stressed-out wife can add stress to your life and further complicate your home environment and your relationship with your partner.

Early on in your career as an at-home dad, sit down with your wife and create a schedule of when each of you can take breaks, either alone or together. Explain to your wife that it is important to have these breaks so that you can devote more energy and time to the kids and be the father that you want to be without feeling resentful. And encourage your partner to take these personal breaks, too, for the same reasons. The last thing anyone wants is a burned-out primary caregiver who hates being at home with the kids—that will not benefit anyone.

My antidote to burnout is an annual men's fishing weekend. My brother-in-law, Ken, initiated this trip for my brother Charles and me. We go to northern Maine once a year for a long weekend, with no kids and no wives. We spend the entire time in his Nitro motorboat, basically goofing off from dawn to dusk. It's the most "me time" fun I have all year, and by the time the trip is over, I'm missing my family and am excited to be reunited with them (even if I never catch any fish). If you're not lucky enough to have a men's fishing weekend, then any routine activity with your buddies will do the job.

Whether it is going to the movies with your buddies or going for a jog or a round of golf, try to find something you enjoy doing and go out and do it once a month. Make a schedule of out-of-the-house activities that you could do once a month and talk to your wife about what is feasible. Obviously a weekend away once a month may not be doable, but a movie with your friends every month, while scheduling a weekend away once or twice a year, should be workable.

VCRs and PVCs

What do Jell-O and VCRs have in common? Nothing—unless you are two years old. If there is any Jell-O left over from dessert, it usually ends up in the VCR. Other combinations are dangerous, like screwdrivers and electrical outlets, or just plain messy, like chocolate pudding and your cat. I think you get the point here. To satisfy my son's craving for these scientific experiments, I handed him a pile of leftover one-inch PVC pipe (the white plastic kind for plumbing jobs). It worked! He spent most of the afternoon connecting the elbow joints to the pipes to T-squares to more pipes and made a contraption that could be only found in Dr. Seuss's *Hoober-Bloob Highway* or *Green Eggs and Ham.*

—*Holly Baylies, Stoneham, Massachusetts*

Taking the Kids

While the idea of "me time" may be to get away from the kids, some dads find that their children are just as burned out as they are. While you might be bored and tired of your day-to-day routine, they, too, may be acting up because they want some excitement. A lot of times, just getting out with the kids may be what you all need to feel better about things. One father who discovered this is John Slevens of Berkeley Heights, New Jersey.

I reached the ultimate burnout point this summer. My boys are now thirteen and nine, and the novelty of Dad being home had worn off after my third summer with them. August dragged on and the straw that broke the camel's back came around the first week. My sons (who get up at 8:30 A.M. and 10:30 A.M.) lay around the house, leaving their cereal bowls, clothes, and whatever junk they had lying on the floor. This one particular morning, they started fighting over what to watch on TV. Amid their squalor, I let out a primal scream and said, "I'm sick and tired of being your maid, I spend all day long picking up after both you pigs, and what thanks do I get?" Then like a bolt of lightning it hit: they are bored! All they have to look forward to each day until school is TV, hanging around, and eating. I called my wife immediately and said, "I'm taking the boys to upstate New York and just giving them a good time." She said, "Great idea, they need some father/son time where you're not picking up after them." So we went to upstate New York, got a hotel room in the town of Windham, and then proceeded to have an adventure. I took them go-kart racing, and then we played miniature golf, followed by a water balloon fight. We then went to a mountain stream that empties into a small natural pool and had a hot dog roast over an open fire. I found that I needed a break in the routine, and learned that after you get the chores done, play with the kids! They need it and you need it. I suppose I was trying so hard to be Super Dad I neglected to see that part of being Super Dad is to know when to work hard and when to play.

When my son John was two years old, we would go on errands that I cleverly described as adventure or mystery trips. I would take these adventure trips nearly every day. For several weeks we had a routine in which we would visit the pet store, where he loved to look at the birds, guinea pigs, snakes, and fish. Then on to the fire station, where the crew was always more than happy to talk, and even hoisted John onto the fire truck a few times. Along the way we would come across a crew cutting down a tree or a construction project, and a few times even a fire. This can be a learning experience for you and your kids!

So when you need to get out of the house and out of the rut of your daily life at home *and* you must take the kids, think like a kid and create fun adventures to share. Try to remember what you were interested in at your children's ages, and then find a way to share that thrill. A hike in the woods, a visit to a pet store, a drive to a new part of town (or out of town to an area of rolling pastures)—it doesn't have to cost a thing as long as you expend a bit of your imagination.

Avoiding Burnout at Home

Sometimes, on a cold or rainy day, you just can't get out of the house and the kids might be going stir crazy. At times such as these, you have to do something brainless that both you and your kids like. Curtis Cooper of Shawnee, Kansas, simply watches his favorite cartoon show with the kids. He says, "I watch *SpongeBob SquarePants* daily to keep my inner child intact." (He claims to have ten SpongeBob T-shirts and says, "He's my hero.") At least for that hour he gets his downtime and some big laughs with the kids, and this lowers his stress level in a hurry.

If cartoons aren't for you, try a game or something childlike with your kids. One father I know loves to play video games a few hours a week with his kids. This kind of mindless activity helps him decompress. In the winter, making snowmen or getting into a snowball fight, or in the summer, a watergun fight, may be enough to relieve some of that tension and have some fun with the kids.

Can't take a vacation? At-home dad Steve Rodgers, from Topeka, Kansas, provides the quickest solution to burnout.

> I go into one of the kids' rooms by myself and I lie down in their bed and reminisce about when I was their age. It makes me remember that they are only kids, and it reminds me how much I love them and how fortunate I am to have kids and to be a parent. There is nothing more reassuring than when my son says, "Dad, I love you," right out of the blue, or when my daughter crawls into my lap and kisses me on my cheek and cuddles next to me. I have had burnout dissolve at a record pace in those situations.

Flash Memory

Your kids too wired up for bed? Grab a few flashlights, turn off the lights, and let them run wild through the house for twenty minutes in the dark.

—From the Author

Finding a moment of quiet reflection can help you put things in perspective.

Many dads have found that taking up hobbies or returning to old ones is an effective way to break up the monotony of their routines for themselves and for their children. For example, learning to play a musical instrument is a good way to enjoy your time at home. When I started writing this book, I picked up the guitar again—something I hadn't done since my days in college. I was pretty bad at it, but I found that the challenge of learning new music gave me a rewarding feeling. I eventually found another at-home dad in town who also played, and learning the ropes together, we have a good time! With a guitar you only need to know two to three simple chords to keep your kids entertained. (And if you can find an extra instrument stored in the basement that you don't mind having banged around, let your kids have a little fun, too.) One day I even took out the pots and pans and gave my son a few spoons, and he entertained himself for an hour! If you are pretty stressed out, however, the noise might not help the situation.

Take It in Stride

Another common problem that causes burnout is taking on too much at once. Often dads think that now that they are at home with the kids, they should have extra time to do all of those home projects that they were not able to do because of their office jobs. For example, Casey Spencer of Encino, California, found that he took on too many home projects. With a 109-year-old house he bought the year before his daughter, Keilani, was born, he felt compelled to "do the backyard landscaping, make new wood-frame window screens, improve the ventilation/filter system, make doors for bathroom cabinets, and more." He contends, "Burnout approaches when these conflicting job titles collide with a cranky wife, too many incomplete chores, unread newspapers, and my wife saying she wants us to spend the weekend with her parents! I'm doing a pretty good job at trying to be a saint, just hoping the results are more humility rather than simply exhaustion."

A simple response in this case is just picking a few things out of the "millions of things" you need to do, putting them on a short list, and getting them done today. I also try to add one thing my wife would like me to do, even if it's as simple as something she needs at the store that she may not have time to get, or cleaning a small part of the house that has been cluttered. By planning, many dads find that it's easier to schedule some time outside the home for themselves. Peter Johnson, from Durango, Colorado, notes,

> My son, Jon, is eighteen months old, and at first I didn't go anywhere and saved all of my errands for after my wife got home from work. I was trying to avoid the hassle of packing a bag with diapers, toys, extra clothes, lugging the stroller around, and so on. Now, if I know we're going out in the afternoon, I get everything ready while Jon is eating lunch, confined in his high chair. It really cuts down on, "No, no, don't touch that. Stay away from that. Let go of the cat." It's a welcome break to jump in the car and go to the park for a little swinging and sliding.

Just as fathers can get burned out, kids can, too. A change in routine might not only be manageable, but it might also end up delighting you with a great surprise, such as the first time your child sees a balloon or eats cotton candy.

The most dangerous part of burnout is that you have the tendency to take it out on the kids when it's not their fault. Children will be children, and if you are yelling at them, it will increase the chance that they will start acting up. It's important to remember that most of the time you simply cannot control what is happening around you. You cannot control the inevitable bruises, cuts, Legos in the VCR, or when the kids get sick. When these things all happen at the same time, you have to remember through all the chaos that these things will not change for a while. And if you cannot change it, change the way you think about it. One dad puts it this way:

> Parenting involves sacrifice, and children demand and deserve lots of attention. But if you give them their due, they will fill your life with depth and meaning. It may not be all happiness, but it is the most important work you will ever do.

Being able to look at the big picture may carry you through the most difficult times.

Linen Caves

One thing that my toddler loves to do is climb around in tents and tunnels. So we take blankets, sheets, towels, and more, and spread them over the couches, chairs, and tables to create a cave system throughout the house. He can spend hours moving in and out and just staying in and playing.

—*Jim Mains, Oak Park, Illinois*

In talking to at-home dads over the last ten years, I have asked dads what they have changed for themselves that made for a more stress-free family. Below are ten simple things that you can do to make the household a more pleasant environment:

1. **Talk to them and listen to them.** When your kids know you are listening to them, it makes them realize their input matters, and gives them a feeling of control and self-worth.

2. **Treat them with respect.** When you respect them, they will respect you back.

3. **Give a lot of hugs and kisses.** A feeling of being loved gives your kids a feeling of self-confidence.

4. **Show you love your spouse in front of your kids.** Seeing Mom and Dad show affection toward each other gives them two role models.

5. **Allow kids to be self-reliant.** Let them try things for themselves, no matter how foolish it may seem to you (provided it's safe). For example, my kids liked to do experiments by mixing water with several objects and putting it in the freezer to see what happens. They couldn't wait to see what it would look like the following day. After a while, when we trusted them with the toaster, we encouraged them to make toast. (My oldest son is twelve and is making a pretty good ham and cheese omelet now.)

6. **Communicate with your spouse and agree on parenting styles.** To avoid a public argument and mixed messages, make sure you and your wife agree on your children's behavior.

7. **Get to know your kids' friends.** As your children get older and a few neighborhood kids start to visit, listen to them and learn what they are like and how mature they are. This will give you better judgment when they start asking to do more outside the house.

8. **Don't expect too much, but don't be a pushover.** Pick your battles: some disagreements may not be worth the argument. For

example, if your children want to walk to school without a raincoat, let them do it, and see if the consequences will help them make a better decision next time. But if you have a serious issue, stand by it.

9. **Avoid yelling at them at all costs.** Always discipline with reason, not fear. When you don't like a decision or action your children are making, calmly ask them why they are making the decision. Have them explain what might happen; sometimes they will see why you might be right.

10. **Create as much adventure as possible for your kids.** Creating adventure, although it may not be a popular pastime for the moms, is one way that many at-home dads deal with burnout. This does not mean taking the kids skydiving or white water rafting. It is amazing what adventures you can find within a few blocks of your house. In fact, many dads find that every time they take their children out of the house it can be an adventure.

Getting out of the house to do things together is important not only for your sanity; these times are important bonding experiences. Many at-home dads have incorporated these field trips into their weekly or monthly routines. And their families are better for it.

I hope that this chapter will help you get through some of the more difficult periods of being an at-home dad. In the next chapter, I will look at the inevitable moment when your kids go off to school, leaving you with the decision of how you want to define your new role.

SPOTLIGHT ON DAD
"Field Trips"

BY DAVID EPSTEIN *David Epstein, formerly from Utah, now lives in West Hartford, Connecticut*

Not every outing I've taken my son on has been a success. I figure that if you don't get kicked out of someplace one out of seven trips, you're not trying hard enough.

"All right," I said, running up the white diaper, "we're getting out." I have been getting out of the house since my child was born. My control freak of a spouse was three weeks postpartum when I simply loaded up the baby (and his fifty-three pounds of gear) and left. In her weakened state, she could not protest, so she suffered the consequence: several blissful hours of uninterrupted sleep. Like every expectant couple, we promised one another that we would not let parenting curtail our activities. Boy, were we full of it. But we have managed to keep on going, despite the reality of a tiny person.

All through my son's infancy I continued to take him out. Sometimes I loaded up the lad in a backpack and hiked up above 10,000 feet in the Wasatch Range. Some hikes were idyllic tromps in the mountains, as attested to by my videotaping. Other times the kid howled loudly for mile after mile, obliging the forest rangers to request that I stop terrorizing the wildlife. The meltdowns, too, remain on videotape.

We left the mountains West and now reside in cosmopolitan New England, so the outings are less spectacular. But the outings remain the cornerstone of my parenting. So extensive are my field trips that I have received the highest honor a guy can get: my mother-in-law said that she hopes to be reincarnated as one of my children. Even my own father professed his admiration for my outings program. Where do we go? Everywhere: railroad yards, airports, water plants, industries, and construction sites.

You can have a whole lot of fun if you're willing to take a few risks, push the envelope, ask for things nicely, and take defeat gracefully. I have taken Leo to a tremendous number of places that most kids just don't get to go to. Simply being pushy is a skill I have learned from my wife. Applied to parenting, I combine this aggressive attitude with my experience at teaching juvenile delinquents, where the field trip epitomizes education.

Did someone leave a giant wheel loader on the construction site? Sitting in a massive, dormant machine can be thrilling for a toddler. Does a sign read "No spectators beyond this point?" Remember these four magic words: "He's just a baby." Or simply use the formula "Gosh, I'm sorry, it's just that he loves _____ (fill in the blank). A word to the wise: many places are increasingly aware of their potential liability in the event of an accident. Be smart: don't wander blatantly into a hard-hat area where a lot of huge machines are whipping about. Ask the foreman for a safe place to stand. I always have a "Little Tykes" hard hat in the car with me; put it on a toddler and the construction workers become very friendly.

You can go amazing places by appearing in person and, while holding an idyllic cherub in your arms, asking nicely and smiling a lot. Try to be wearing a clean shirt. Go see things that you want to see. Kids catch enthusiasm like they do colds. If you're a railroad buff, go down to the yards and check out the rolling stock. If you're a newspaper man, a toddler will stare at a spinning press until his eyes fall out. Like heights? Every church janitor has the keys to the steeple. Don't be afraid to bring cameras. Spouses love to see what you do all day.

The payoffs of the field trip mentality are legion. Ever since we visited our local Air National Guard, Leo knows his jets. When a pair of aircraft zips overhead at the playground and every other neander-toddler spouts primitively, "A plane!" my little graduate says keenly, "An A-10!"

One evening my wife wanted to know how Leo learned the word *carillon*. He learned it when a careless park worker left open the back door of the stone tower in which the carillon lives. Quasimodad and his kid had skipped merrily up the bell tower. At the top a ladder disappeared into the heights. The next day I was changing a bulb in the garage ceiling. I turned around to find that a miniature Tenzing Norgay had ascended the ladder and waited at my feet for me to finish negotiating Hillary's Step. My wife observed, "Gee, he went right up that ladder." Sometimes when the baby says something wacko about riding a waterwheel, it's safest to just mumble, "I don't know where he gets that stuff." Truth is, it's amazing that his first words weren't, "Don't tell Mommy!"

8

Is There Life After Kindergarten?

From the moment my son's umbilical cord was snipped, I started the bonding process with him, one that my wife, Sue, had started nine months earlier. But with the cutting of the cord, I realized that John (and later David, my second son) was starting on an independent journey through life. The first milestone happened a few weeks after John's cord was cut, when the leftover part fell off and created his belly button. I saved his skin in a plastic baggie, maybe as a way of preserving the moment. This didn't work out too well, since it now looks like a raisin.

As the years passed, my sons outgrew more things that they needed as infants, such as the Jolly Jumper, the formula bottles, the high chair, and, later, the playpen. These things were first moved to the basement and later converted into cash at our yard sale, where we shared them with other young families. Every time something like a high chair or playpen would disappear, it was a milestone to me, a milestone that indicated that my boys were slowly becoming less dependent on my wife and me. The next milestone was the crib; it left our family once David learned how to climb out of it. I shared the job of dismantling it with my boys, who seemed to enjoy this project, especially when I gave them the chance to use my screwdrivers for the first time.

After it was disassembled, I put the pieces of the crib and the mattress at the top of the stairs so I could take it out to the garbage. And something completely unexpected happened: my then six-year-old son, John, grabbed the mattress and his younger brother, put the mattress at the top of the stairs with the two of them on top of it, and rode it down to the bottom. Since it was too late for me to grab him, all I could do was watch as they happily careened down the stairs. (John had gotten the idea from the movie *Home Alone* when Macaulay Culkin took a toboggan down his stairs.) Thankfully the kids didn't get hurt, and although I was scared and angry that John did something so stupid, I was secretly proud that he made an independent (and creative) decision and took a risk—another step toward independence.

The day finally came when John boarded the bus that would take him to preschool. It wasn't so bad as I turned around to head back home, since I still had one-year-old David with me. But when it was David's turn to board that bus, I was left all alone. I stood there stunned and sad as the bus drove away, wondering, "What am *I* supposed to do now?" With my first taste of time alone at home since I had kids, I experienced something most dads do when they have their first day home alone, a mixed feeling of freedom and sadness. During the endless days of changing diapers, I remember sometimes longing for my days of freedom again. But be prepared: once it comes, you may end up with a preview of the empty nest syndrome. With the house empty and strangely quiet for five to six hours, you will be asking yourself some questions about your new role at home.

In this chapter I explore such questions as:

- Should you seek employment outside of the home?
- Are you still an at-home dad?
- If you stay home, is your role still important to your wife and children?

Backyard Pinball

While playing ball in a neighbor's yard with a big slope, I got the idea to turn the backyard into a huge pinball machine. With help from my neighborhood friend Ben and my brother, John, I spent the entire day scattering old toys, barrels, buckets, and pieces of wood through-out the yard as targets to kick a ball at. I then devised a point system whereby points are accumulated for each target hit, or each barrel or bucket kicked. Each player gets two balls to kick. You keep playing until the ball goes out of bounds. (We create our own out-of-bounds with rope). After all the kick balls are used, tally up your points. Who-ever gets the most points after three rounds wins.

The most difficult target I created is a toilet plunger. I stuck this upside down in the ground. If you are able to get the ball to land in it, you get 200 points. (After a week, no one has done it yet!) This game combines creativity with math.

—David Baylies, age nine, North Andover, Massachusetts

- What will your typical day be like now if you work or stay home?
- What will the reaction from others be if you continue to stay home?

What Should You Do Now?

What to do after your kids start school is one of the hardest deci-sions you may make. Some fathers who initially decided to stay home are no longer sure if they are still at-home dads. Researcher Dr. Robert Frank suggests that at-home dads should ask themselves the following questions:

- Do you still do household chores during the day?
- Are you there when your children come home from school?
- Do you care for them until your wife comes home?

If the answer is mostly yes, then you are still an at-home dad, since you are still your children's primary caregiver. Of course, other questions may come to mind, taking into account this change in your children's needs.

- Should you get a part-time/full-time job outside or in the house?
- Do your kids still need you at home?
- What are your needs now?
- How have they changed from when you first made the decision to be an at-home dad?

Even if you have answers to all of these questions, the right choice for you may not be so clear.

Casey Spencer of Los Angeles, California, described how he wrestled with this issue when it was time for him to make this decision.

Let's face it, it isn't easy to convince myself or my wife that we "need" me to be home as much as I am now. After all, if my girl is away at school four hours a day, don't I owe it to my family to at least edge my way back into "productive" (i.e., "paid") work? The guilt is eating at me because I don't think this will be easy to confront. It might just be easier to stop making a joke about how I'll be sitting in the back of all her classes and make it a plan. In reality, I hope very strongly that I can afford the luxury we have now, one that allows me to devote all of my time to my family and none to breadwinning. I anticipate a new round of embarrassment ("What do

---

Udder Disaster?

What do you call a cow that jumps over a barbed wire fence? An udder disaster. While we are on the subject, here's my four-year-old son's favorite art project from his preschool. Make your kid a farmer. Get a pair of those rubber gloves from the pediatrician's office. Fill them with white water-soluble paint, lay out some construction paper, and squeeze the finger so that the paint (milk) squirts out to create an "udder painting," or udder disaster.

—From the Author

---

you do all day while your kid is at school?"), yet at the same time I anticipate that our family would benefit from the contributions I can make that are on hold right now, as well as the benefits in being closely involved in my girl's schooling.

This moment of transition is very hard for many stay-at-home dads.

Steve Klem of Cocoa Beach, Florida, already made up his mind to stay home instead of returning to work. He says,

I had made no real plans as to what would happen when the kids went to school. One of the things I missed as a kid was having involved parents in my life. As early as I can remember, we were always doing the latchkey thing. I used to hate coming home to an empty house, and worse yet, I hated staying at school. I don't want that kind of environment for my kids. Even though they may not always come home, I want them to know that home will be the sanctuary for them that it should be.

The experience of these fathers highlights a number of things you need to consider when making the decision whether to go back to work or not. First of all, do you want to go back to work? Are there opportunities that you want to take advantage of? Sit down and talk to your wife about the pros and cons of your going back to work. At the same time, think about how each choice may affect your relationship with your kids. It may be that you can gradually transition back into the working world by starting out part-time. If you have the luxury of orchestrating a slow transition, then that may be ideal for you and your family. Like any decision, weigh the benefits of going back to work versus staying at home. And maybe, too, there is a happy compromise by which you can work two days a week, or some other formula that meets everyone's needs. The important thing is to realize that your needs and those of your family are constantly changing as your children grow and as your needs and your wife's needs change. Take time to assess your current needs—emotional, personal, financial—and then make a decision that best meets these needs.

When You Stay at Home

As this book goes to print, I have one boy in the fourth grade and another in the seventh. Although our income is less, I remain glad about my decision to stay home. The main reason? I feel that my kids need me more than ever as they close in on their teenage years. It's great to be able to be home when they come home, and they can tell me about their day while it is still fresh in their minds. They always have some questions to ask me about their homework or something that happened at school. You can't buy that kind of personal attention that your kids need.

One dad from Minnesota found—through experience—that staying at home was better for both him and his family, even after his kids got older.

I've been home better than fifteen years starting with the birth of my first child. I assumed I'd return to the workforce, but when I tried, our family life deteriorated rapidly and all members (including myself) wanted me back home. The needs of our children change over time, but never to the point of my not being needed. Now that my children are fifteen and eleven, I feel they need me as much as ever. Not on the daily stuff like being fed and clothed so much as providing a loving ear and gentle guidance. I have a great relationship with my kids, and find that topics they have on their minds are very difficult subjects for them to deal with alone. It's reassuring to know they can come to me rather than their peers.

Luckily for him, he was able to realize this and make the choice to return to the role of at-home dad.

Rick Andrews of Cincinnati, Ohio, decided to continue to be an at-home dad as his son, Nick, prepared for preschool.

While at home, I ended up doing overdue chores that seemed to go very quickly. I completed them all without one interruption from Nicky. I didn't have to negotiate where to move the kitchen chairs so the floor could be mopped, or, for that matter, worry about how hot the water in the mop bucket was so he could play in it. I actually got some painting done on our new door framing without having a nightmarish mess to clean up. There was no in-between time when flowers got pulled up or when the sandbox got turned into a mess. At the same time there was not one second when that little face and lovable grin was not first and foremost in my mind today!

I had the same experience as Andrews—more time to clean the house and do errands without taking care of the kids at the same time. Although I missed the kids, losing the juggling act was nice.

Yes, But Does the Bell Work with Cows?

When my son was five years old, he started playing at a friend's house next door. When dinnertime arrived, we ran over to call him. Well, now we have stumbled onto an old solution. When I was young, my mom would call me to dinner simply by ringing an old cowbell that she got from her grandmother. I would come running home every time.

We have inherited this cowbell from my mom and tried it when we needed my son for supper, whether he is in the house or down the street a full block away. To our amazement, he comes running the second he hears that bell, just like I used to.

—From the Author

I didn't take on a new outside job, and would recommend waiting a few weeks or months before taking on a new job. When planning for your kids-at-school days, set a schedule for yourself and try to stick to it. See if in that schedule you could fit enough time for a hobby or part-time job that won't overload you or shortchange your family time.

To give you a better idea of a typical day at home with your kids in school, I asked Frank Harrison of Dallas, Texas, to provide us with a glimpse of his day while his son was in the first grade.

6:30	Wake and prepare breakfast and lunch for Dylan.
7:20	Bring Dylan to the bus stop.
8:00 to 10:00	Walk dog and exercise.
10:00 to 12:00	Volunteer at school.
12:15 to 2:45	Errands and chores (shopping, housecleaning).
3:00	Pick up Dylan and four friends to be dropped off at Cub Scouts. Not my turn to stay and help. Free time till 4:30.

4:30	Take dog for second mandatory walk of day. Go to pick up Dylan at Scouts since they're running late. I get to sit in the truck and read a magazine (quiet time).
5:00	Home again, Dylan needs snack and to change into soccer clothes for special practice.
5:30	Had to stay and help. Kicked soccer balls.
6:30	Home again. Wife still at work so no rush to fix dinner. Homework is started; have to sit at table with him for support and help (get to finish magazine). Fix dinner.
6:50	Wife comes home. Eat dinner together.
7:30	Finish eating and do dishes while wife spends quality snuggle time with Dylan on couch.
8:00	Practice my computer class lessons.
8:30	Dylan is officially put to bed and read to by my wife.

As this schedule shows, Frank used his extra time wisely by mixing volunteer schoolwork, alone time, and home time with the family. By balancing his schedule so that he had plenty of adult conversation during the day, he steers clear of the feelings of isolation and keeps his sanity as his wife goes through her workday (which can often carry on into her evenings). Also, this schedule shows the importance of continuing to share responsibilities with your spouse. It may be easy for you and your wife to assume that since you have all this extra time on your hands, everything should be covered by you. But this is not true—you need to discuss with your wife what you hope to achieve in your day now that the kids are at school and how she can help.

Many dads find that school often offers a realm of opportunities for them to stay involved with their kids. Scott Manifold of Columbus, Ohio, reports, "I've gotten into room parenting for Alex's class. I even got to organize this year's holiday party. Alex's teacher was surprised at having a dad so involved, but I've noticed that the majority of parents that pick up the kids are the dads."

Returning to Work

After the discussions and evaluations, many dads do decide that going back to work is the best option. One of those dads was Phil Isis of Greeley, Colorado, who says, "We are now once again a two-income family. A good friend of mine just happened to need help with his property maintenance business. Talk about spontaneous timing. I started out part-time but have since gone full time and everything is working great. I have enough flexibility to pick up my youngest from school and go to all soccer games and practices. I also still do the laundry, housecleaning, shopping, and the never-ending landscaping project on our home. Old habits are hard to break."

However, of course not all fathers are lucky enough to have a work opportunity waiting in the wings for them. Jack Simpson of Nashville, Tennessee, struck an ominous note for those thinking of returning to work after an extended stay at home. After fourteen years of raising his daughter, he couldn't find a job and returned to school to earn his MBA. He notes, "The problem seems to be that employers believe that if you haven't worked at a paying job in a number of years, you can't be serious about wanting to return to work." He offers the following advice, "Once your kids are old enough to go to school, then you can start school yourself, even if only for half a day. Employers need to see that you have kept your skills current."

The idea of going back to an office—any office—may be terrifying, especially if it has been several years since you have been in the working world. Obviously, the more you plan ahead for your return to work, the better. If you always have a feeling in the back of your head that you may want to go back to work someday, keep up with your old job—your old contacts, colleagues—and try to

Toothbrush Reporter

My seven-year-old, Liza, used to hate brushing her teeth. Not any more! One night, I picked up a comb and began talking into it. "Dan Dunsmore here, and we're in Liza Dunsmore's bathroom this evening to witness an incredible act. Liza is going to brush her teeth just exactly the way her mom and dad have suggested." I gave a blow-by-blow account, and she began playing to the imaginary crowd of onlookers who had gathered to gawk, and to the television audience to whom I was reporting. I continued, "Liza is now making sure she is brushing up and down, not sideways. Oops! Looks as if she may have missed one. Liza, would you like to make a comment at this time?" Of course, at this point, her mouth is totally full of toothpaste foam, so she spits some of it everywhere as she breaks into laughter. With foam in her mouth, she mumbles about what a proud moment this is for her. As she prepares to spit out the rest of the paste, I continued: "Ladies and gentlemen, Liza is about to spit! Let's see if she's able to hit the sink." Liza and I laugh as she rinses.

—Dan Dunsmore, Charlottesville, Virginia

take any training/classes that will help you keep up-to-date on how your field has advanced during your time away. The more you can show potential employers that you have maintained your interest in your field, the more receptive they will be. If they just see a five- or six-year gap in your resume, they may not be prone to calling you in for an interview.

Remember, if you have high unemployment in your area, it may take a while to get a job once you have made your decision to work outside the house. Networking and informational interviews, when you just call places where you want to work and ask to meet with the top executives, are good starters here. Checking in with your friends and the parents of your children's friends for potential opportunities may also be helpful. Other at-home parents in particular, who will be empathetic to your situation, could be an asset if they have contacts in the field you want to pursue. You may want to look up some career counselors—check the yellow pages or the local university to see what resources they can offer you.

One solution to keeping employed is to work at home. Many dads feel a need to work in some capacity, and have been able to work part- or even full-time jobs at home with their kids. Right now, this is the solution I have chosen for myself. While my kids are at school, I work on this book and the at-home dad Web site. When they come home, I'm around to play with them and get dinner ready. (For more on working at home, read Chapter 6 to learn about at-home dads who have been able to earn an income while staying home with their children.)

As this chapter has shown, each new phase of being an at-home dad will present new challenges. In the final section before the resources, I will offer a series of personal stories from at-home dads.

SPOTLIGHT ON DAD
"Driving Away"
BY MARK DAVID SCHAEFER *Mark David Schaefer lives in Los Angeles, California.*

I left the car idling in the middle of the Sunday-empty parking lot of the Federal Building while we switched places. Rachael's permit was in the glove compartment. Her plan was to get her license as soon as possible after her sixteenth birthday. That gave us just over six months. She pulled the seat forward and adjusted the mirrors while I got my seat belt on. It was my first time in the passenger seat of my own car. I nodded. She watched her own hand make three distinct steps from park, to reverse, to neutral, and then into drive. She put her hands at ten and two and, slowly, we rolled forward.

We did OK that first day, starting in the parking lot before moving on to small neighborhood streets. I tried to appear calm, and did not yell once or show panic. I didn't know what to do with my hands. I opted to dig my fingernails right into the vinyl of the armrest and kept the left hovering between the emergency brake and the underside of the steering wheel. I have no idea if the hand brake would have stopped the car, and I only had to grab the wheel once or twice. I still wonder if Rachael noticed that at every intersection I pressed my feet hard enough into the floor to rear myself up the back of the seat.

She had trouble at first with the turns. She'd take them wide, trying to keep her hands on the wheel, getting her arms crossed, ending up on the left side of the road while I clenched every muscle in my body. Then she'd career back to the right. My Geo Prizm never felt so large. The parked cars all seemed very close from my perspective. Everything appears too close and 20 MPH feels like 40 (and 40 feels like Mach 1) when your child is driving. I kept wondering if I should say something, something more than, "You're doing fine. Straighten it out. Stop. That's a stop sign. Stop! It's OK. Just back up slowly." I wondered if there was some lecture I should have been delivering through it all. I couldn't think of anything for a while, and so I just rode along, clutching the armrest and cramping my legs until out of nowhere Rachael said, "I don't know why they have all these mirrors. I never use them." I explained how useful mirrors can be, recalling as I did how disorienting they were to me at first. And then I explained blind spots. And the techniques of defensive driving. And watching out for pedestrians. And bicyclists. And people getting out of parked cars. And animals. And anything else I could think of that moves.

We drove for nearly an hour. Rachael was excited, but also serious and, I think, a little intimidated, as she should've been. She kept her hands at ten and two. She looked left, then right, then left again, before inching through intersections. She had to look down now and again to find the right pedal, and she once hit the gas when she meant the brake. All in all, though, she drove slowly and somewhat evenly, and we didn't hit anything, and nothing hit us. Rachael's the only other person to have ever driven my car, and since her mother never took her out, with the exception of the three two-hour lessons with the driving school instructors, I am the only person she's ever driven with. I will always be surprised by how far forward she has to pull the driver's seat. In order for me to get into the car after she's been driving, I have to slide in sideways and push the seat back to make room for my legs. I remember asking her early on if she could see the hood of the car when she drives. She assured me she can, but still, she seems just plain too small to be driving. I couldn't have been so small, so young when I got my license.

We drove together for seven months. We started on the small neighborhood lanes and then moved on to the busier streets. Eventually, I let her have the radio on while she drove, and, later, even let her change the stations herself. We backed up a lot. We parked. We parked again. We got honked at and glared at a few times. We drove at night. We drove in the rain. We even went on the freeway. By the end, I could rest my hands in my lap. I even risked a look at the scenery now and again. Eventually, I became just a passenger, and she the driver.

By the time today arrives, she is ready. I am sitting on a cold, cement bench outside the DMV while the examiner gets into my car and quizzes Rachael on the location of the lights, the defroster, on hand signals. My daughter has long been anticipating the independence of driving herself to school, to parties, to friends' homes. I'll be able to sleep later in the morning. I'll get home from work earlier. I'll have more time to myself. Still, though, I'll miss having her in the car. She lives with me only every other weekend, but I've driven her to and from school every day since kindergarten. We've had breakfast in the car, and snacks. We've done homework in the car. She's told me about what she's reading, about her best friends and her worst enemies. When she was younger, she'd slouch in the passenger seat and prop her feet up on the dashboard. In just the right sunlight, I could see multiple imprints from her shoe treads on the windshield. In that car we've discussed the triumphs and catastrophes of elementary school, middle school, and now high school. We've discussed world events in my Prizm. Those rides to and from school kept me in touch with who my daughter was, with who she is, and I'm about to lose that precious car time. She'll have friends to see, parties to attend, boys to date. She'll be driving.

And someday, whether she realizes it yet or not, she will hit something, or something will hit her. It's inevitable. If we're lucky, her first accident will be a simple fender bender, unnerving, but without any injuries. Still, she will stand on the side of the road, while traffic whizzes by, frightened, distraught, probably in tears. The other driver will probably be an adult, and will probably ooze disdain for my daughter and for all teenage drivers. My Rachael will apologize again and again, even if it's not wholly her fault, and she will tremble and struggle to give coherent information. I can't escape the fact that someday my daughter will be alone, and frightened, and I will be someplace else, at work, or at home, unavailable, unaware. The in-car quiz is over, and it's time to drive. Rachael looks over her left shoulder and, with the grim and terse examiner in my seat, she pulls out. I've taught her as best I can. There's nothing more I can do. I can't take the test for her. I can't ride along. I can only watch as she drives away, out of sight.

From the Frontlines of Fatherhood: More Dads in the Spotlight

I hope you have enjoyed reading this book as much as I have enjoyed writing it. I would like to end it by sharing the following stories from at-home dads, including one about myself. Whether humorous or heartfelt, I think these final accounts will help you with your own experiences at the frontlines of fatherhood.

"Moving to the Multi-Child Family"

BY DAVID EPSTEIN *David Epstein lives in West Hartford, Connecticut.*

Remember the board game Life? You landed on a certain square and were told to "add a child." You took a blue or a pink peg and jammed it into your little plastic car (no safety seat required), collected your bonus bucks, and went on with the game. Simple, right? We just added a child, a pink peg, and it's anything but simple. This adding stuff, which is called multiplying in the Bible—go figure—is like gearing up to run a marathon. Remember the first time you added a child? You wanted to go to the store with the baby and it took you two days to get out of the house. With practice, that was soon down to forty-five minutes. Now you're a pro and you can get out of the house with a child in about ten minutes. Once upon a time, that would have seemed downright reckless. Ten minutes would have meant that you forgot something really crucial, probably the baby.

Our new addition has been here for seven months already, so our marital bliss has resurfaced. We no longer have an excuse for the condition of the pigsty we inhabit, and I can get out of the house with both kids in about fifteen minutes. One of the most important things to keep in mind when having a second child is that moving to a multi-child family requires a major attitude adjustment. One child can be made to conform to your life. Two children tip the balance to where the children now rule. The trick is never to let them know that. Offspring can sense stress the same way they can sense a sphincter relaxing; it brings them on like bloodthirsty sharks. You can't bottle-feed the baby and spoon-feed the mush without at least three hands, and your third and fourth hands are still asleep. Result: stress. Learn to respond to chaos by smiling and gently nodding. Where have you seen this behavior? Right: senility. Now you know where it comes from. Don't mourn; just redefine your terms. Instead of "good," go for "good enough."

Your goal as the house spouse is to see that everyone under your care survives. Some guys think that the day's goal is to occupy both children long enough to read the sports page. I like to think that a better goal is to have achieved everything on a basic daily list. My list runs like this:

1. Nobody is dead.
2. No injuries occurred that required much more treatment than sympathy, hugs, and kisses.
3. Enough food was eaten to allow individuals to sleep easily through the night.
4. Diapers were changed either when necessary or just to prove daddy is the boss.

Once you've adjusted your attitude to the multi-child family, there are some tools that will help. Strollers are great. We bought one when we had our first child. Now we own at least five, the others being hand-me-downs. Every now and then the baby rides in one, but for the most part, a stroller is just the cart for all your gear; go for the double stroller right off. Yes, a stroller can serve as a high chair in which to feed the baby, but in reality, you can't get through an airport without a stroller to carry all your bags. Babies are easy to carry; you don't have enough hands for all the other stuff.

So you need a baby carrier. As your child grows, you'll use them in this order: sling, frontpack, and backpack. Before you go anywhere, figure out what your needs are. If your older child loves riding escalators at the mall, you can forget about using a stroller. Species that use strollers on escalators will eventually get weeded out by natural selection. A carrier allows you to carry your baby while your toddler zooms along out front. And if you're careful, that toddler will never figure out that you honestly can't catch him while you're wearing that baby.

The sling is a simple device that you will learn to launder often, because it will smell like a combination of your junior high gym locker and a rag soaked in spoiled milk. For very young babies, the sling gives head support and keeps your hands free, one of which will hold a bottle. Your other hand will be free to (a) catch falling toddlers, and (b) mysteriously caress the outside of the sling exactly like a pregnant lady does with her belly. A baby in a sling will sleep. Period. You haul 'em upright to feed 'em, you settle 'em in afterward, and sleep happens. Doubt me? Put the baby into a sling and start vacuuming: Voilà! Dreamland.

Frontpacks are good for very small babies who can hold their heads up. An advantage is that you feel about as close to your child as your wife did during her pregnancy. A disadvantage is that it feels like you're wearing a hot water bottle. One of the best front carriers I've ever used is the "Carry-U," which is produced by moms doing piecework in the hinterlands of Utah. This ingenious rag allows a baby to be gently strapped to your chest facing forward. You can do just about anything while baby ogles his or her favorite person: the older sibling. Snugli and Infantino are among the more commercial variations on the Carry-U.

If your second child is older than about six or eight months, you can use a backpack. These are great because they put the weight on your hips. And if you can move faster than Mach I, you won't hear the whining behind you. The good thing about backpacks is that you can really go places with one. You can hike anywhere: playgrounds, mountains, shopping malls. There are three drawbacks, however. First, when your kid takes off his or her hat, you need to make nice with a stranger to get the hat back on (tip: tether hats and pacifiers to the backpack with short pieces of parachute cord and safety pins). Second, any sudden, loud vocalizations do to your ear what staring at the sun does to your eyes. Third, crumbs go right down your back. That being said, until a kid hits about twenty-five to thirty pounds, the backpack is the ultimate cruiser. Beyond thirty pounds, you'll need a hip replacement.

With just about every baby carrier, you'll have to face the burning question: How do I look in pastels? But there is a growing market for baby carriers for men. I've noticed several new products on the market of late. Snugli is coming out with a front pack that disguises your baby as a Milwaukee tumor. Named "The Baby Gut," I've seen this one on the racks at baseball stadiums and in Home Depot. It even comes with a belt that has a computer-generated graphic at the rear that looks precisely like plumber's cleavage. It comes with a baby bottle disguised as a cold Budweiser.

Aside from carriers, for those of you still living in the nineteenth century, there's a new tool that you really ought to try: the headset cordless phone. Imagine being able to talk with other adults, use both hands at the same time, and not have a permanent crick in your neck. Yeah, you thought you were cool with your cordless telephone, walking out to the mailbox, or taking the trashcans out to the street one at a time. Get real: both hands free. Headset. Radio Shack: $10. Need I say more?

"The Best Father's Day Gift of All"

BY JOHN C. O'BRIEN *John C. O'Brien lives in Scituate, Massachusetts. He returned to the working world after eighteen years as an at-home dad.*

The other day my two children asked me if I wanted anything special for Father's Day, and I was proud not to divulge my powerful yearning for a month in Bermuda alone with my wife. Instead, I said I'd think about their question, and since then, I've been reminiscing about the past eighteen years of my life. I remember being charmed by a young daughter who was capable of telling stories only if they contained countless "um"s and "ah"s and ended with an, "Oh, never mind," accompanied by a crooked smile. I remember my young son trying so hard for instantaneous communication that his words at times became difficult to understand. Rainstorms were "pourdowns" and bunches of flowers were "buffets." During the many football games we played in the backyard, all his touchdowns were scored in the "ozone," and even now, when he passes a group of amateur golfers on the fairway, he feels compelled to warn them of potential flying balls by screaming out "Fort!"

There were many mornings when my daughter made me tea with a set of cups and saucers she had received for her second birthday. Her chin was always set seriously and her pinkies pointed outward to their fullest extent as she poured portions of nonexistent liquid from the kettle. The amusement that flashed from her eyes on those mornings was pristine as she realized, time and time again, that even someone as old as her father still made the mistake of smacking noisily while pretending to eat the invisible muffins she served. My son, on his second birthday, was given a toy lawnmower that made mechanical sounds and produced a slew of bubbles whenever it was pushed. These unique features soon wore out, but there was no question that for the next three years, I could always count on being followed by an enthusiastic junior landscaper—brrrmm-ming away—every time I cut the lawn. In my early years at home, I spent hours and hours wrestling with the flips, curls, side parts, and braids in my daughter's hair. I still feel proud that at least on some days, I was able to send her off to school with a style that looked as if it had some connection to the latter half of the twentieth century.

The dresses she favored at the time had only one requirement: that they lift in symmetrical swirls when she spun in an endless succession of pirouettes. In public, any style of shoe was fine. In private, she preferred large, clunky size 10s, which coincidentally was the size I also wore. One of the few certainties in her life was that she would name her first child "Forsythia Rose."

My son, in his early years, dedicated himself to discovery. He investigated the workings of hinges so constantly that the rest of us would dare walk through a doorway with only the greatest of care. Despite my advice, he felt obliged to find out for himself just how painful a bee sting was, and a week later, not totally certain of the process that had occurred, to suffer a second jolt during a renewed round of research. By the age of 2½, he had developed, through boyish charm and a collection of affable smiles, the ability to work a roomful of adults like a politician on recess from Congress. By means of a method I cannot comprehend, he has fleeced millions of Monopoly dollars from me during poker games in which, always, aces, deuces, one-eyed jacks, itchy kings, and bedpost queens are wild. His agonies and ecstasies have enabled me to live through the events of my own youth a second, more philosophical time.

I remember playing the role of the Tooth Fairy as I made many late-night forays into the bedrooms of both children while fumbling with molars and crumpled dollar bills; seeing Christmas trees that had been toppled by toddlers grasping for ornaments that sparkled too brightly to be resisted; taking the strenuous bike rides up mammoth hills that inexplicably influenced the child riding in the seat behind me to sing the ninety-eighth version of the alphabet song. There is the clammy clutch of tiny hands to remember, and the smell of milky breath; the slipperiness of small, pudgy bodies in baths, and the coldness of feet snuggling into a parents' bed after the nightmares have struck; the pure smiles of achievement, and the times when the intrusion of pain caused hugs so intense, it seemed my son or daughter wanted to climb right inside my body.

I think of these aspects of my life during the past eighteen years and realize that the Father's Day gift I have already received from my children far exceeds any item available in stores today. But still, if they really insisted, I wouldn't refuse that month in Bermuda with my wife.

"Okey Dokey Smokey Pokey Lokey"

BY JOHN WISE *John Wise has been home with his son, Jack, and daughter, Ellen Grace, since June 1994. He now runs his wife's business, Medical Staffing Services of Maine, out of his Brunswick, Maine, home.*

Sometimes I wonder where the little kid in me has gone. Somewhere along the line, my inner child decided to hide. As a matter of fact, he has been resting for as long as I can remember. It has not been until recently that he has shown some signs of life. As a daycare provider and home dad of two wonderful children, the little kid, or Johnny, as I like to call him, comes to life not often enough. I spend much of my time being John. John makes sure the house is clean, the laundry is done, the dishes are put away, lunch is made, snacks are provided, the kids are following the rules, the kids don't kill each other, the money is collected, the receipts are written, the bank is visited, the files are straight, the licenses are up to date, the house is up to code, the food is nutritious. My goodness, the list is endless.

On the other hand, let's give Johnny some credit where it is due. The other day I became very conscious of the fact that I rarely talk like an adult. This, of course, is not a revelation. Dads and moms have been baby-talking since the age of, well, babies. The butchering of the English language is a sure sign that Johnny is alive and kicking. I have found myself replacing the expression "OK" with "okey dokey." It gradually deteriorates to "okey dokey smokey," and finally "okey dokey smokey pokey lokey nokey." My three-year-old's name is Ellen Grace. When she was born, my mother-in-law asked if she could call her Ellie for short. I would have nothing to do with that. Ellen Grace was too pretty a name to be cut into pieces. Three years later, I have managed to mangle the most beautiful name in the world. Ellen Grace has become El, Ellie (don't tell), Lou, Loulee, oolee, oolee kaboolee, ookee poohkee, and loulee kaboolee. My son Jack is Jacka whacka, smackers, Bud Stafanski, Buddy, and boody.

There are more signs that Johnny lives: I love to take the kids to the toy store. When no one is looking, I race down the electronic truck aisle pushing the buttons on all the motorcycles, ambulances, fire trucks, helicopters, and police cars I can find. I do have some rules, though. The kids *must* stay in the cart—makes for a faster getaway. Unfortunately, John takes over when the kids want to play the same game. I'm working on it. John also used to be ever-present during art-time. God forbid things get messy while the kids play with paint, play dough, and glue. I used to have rules about art. Can you believe that? RULES about art? There should never be rules about art. Johnny does not have rules about art. If the floor is a mess, John will clean it up later.

Restaurant John makes sure his kids are acting like kids are supposed to act at a restaurant. Johnny lets his kids strip the top half off the paper straw cover and blow the other half across the dining area. John makes sure the order is nutritious. Johnny orders an extra side of fries. John orders milk all the time. Johnny has the waitperson serve up Hawaiian Punch from time to time. John hates to wait in line, anywhere. He is especially impatient at eating establishments. Johnny tries to make the best of the situation. You may even see Johnny strike up a conversation with the person next to him. This, of course, is unthinkable to John. The only thing worse, according to John, than a slow waitperson is an overly helpful waitperson. When Johnny is around, neither of these people bother him a bit. On rare occasions Johnny might even get his own coffee. John would sulk.

Johnny does not believe in time out. He never uses it. He believes in consequences of actions. If a child is misbehaving, it is his or her way of telling John that she/he is not getting some sort of need met. It is up to Johnny to find out what is wrong. It takes patience, understanding, and listening, along with lots and lots and lots of holding. Johnny has lots of these tools in reserve. John needs to shop around a little more. There are thousands of people, places, and situations John faces every day. They could all be handled quite simply by Johnny. John tends to complicate things. Johnny simplicates. (John, by the way, would never use a non-word like *simplicates*). John is a worrier. Johnny doesn't sweat the small stuff. John takes control. Johnny lets it go. John questions his faith. Johnny never doubts. Please don't misunderstand me. John is a nice guy. Johnny, though, is a *swell* guy.

"A Six Pack for Dad," a profile of Keith Dilley

BY PETER BAYLIES *Keith Dilley is an at-home dad from Indianapolis, Indiana, who became America's most famous father when his wife, Becki, came home in 1993 with sextuplets— that's six newborns! At the time, these babies were America's first surviving sextuplets. I interviewed Dilley in 1993. His children are now eleven-year-olds.*

Keith's previous salary-paid job was as a manager of a restaurant. He and Becki decided that he should stay home for economic reasons, since his wife had the higher-paying job as a nurse. Since they both were home for the first two months, Keith was able to ease into his new role as a super-daddy. When Becki finally returned to work after two months with twelve-hour shifts, he became a full-fledged at-home dad.

The pressure to do well the first week was high, since he had zero experience raising children and he was sailing in uncharted waters. During our interview, Dilley noted that his wife was unsure if he could handle the load. His wife said at one point, "If you do anything wrong, I'll clobber you!" Of his relatives he says, "They were wondering if I could pull it off, but I was glad to prove I could." He notes, "The hardest part was trying to keep the six all happy at the same time. Although I had to really work at it, I learned how to do the job."

His advice to fathers of twins or even triplets is to make sure they are on a schedule. "When one gets up, they all get up, and they all go to bed for naps and bedtime at the same time." (They currently take a two-hour nap from 12:00 to 2:00 each afternoon). Since his wife now works the 2 P.M. to midnight shift during the weekdays, Dilley gets help from his wife during the morning hours getting the four girls and two boys up, bathed, and fed. "The bath time takes an hour, and that's rushing it," Dilley says. The first big milestone for Keith and Becki was the night all six slept through the night—he even remembers the date as if it were a holiday—April 23 of this year (1993). It happened one month after they moved into their new home to accommodate Brenda, Ian, Julian, Quinn, Claire, and Adrian (in order of birth). Now for the first time in nearly a year, the entire Dilley family finally had a good night's sleep. Before the babies slept though the night, the couple would work two shifts caring for the babies. Many times they had to check sensors to monitor any nighttime breathing problems. Even if they managed to get five hours of sleep, they were thankful. Keith still has to get up at 6 A.M., when the babies wake up for another day. They now keep the four girls in one room and the two boys in another.

When his wife leaves at 2 P.M. to go to her nursing job, he starts another afternoon routine of playing, feeding, changing diapers, and putting them to bed at 8 P.M. During the nighttime routine, Dilley sits in the middle of the floor and has them all sit in a circle—he reads to them, and they all go to bed. "They are actually pretty easy since they know the routine. Now they are beginning to protest a little bit. Dilley is unsure what lies ahead for him. "They are now starting to walk and talk a little, and that presents some new problems." He says now he is beginning to have trouble even leaving the room for a minute, since they begin to get separation anxiety. "They will all start crying, but I know that's normal for that age." In the first month, the babies needed forty-two bottles, forty diaper changes, and three loads of laundry each day. This amounted to $40/day for diapers and formula. "The expense of the diapers is really killing us now, it can really add up, as we are still using two packs every day." Of course, the next big milestone will be when all six are toilet-trained. His pediatrician recommended waiting until they are eighteen months before they start learning about bathrooms. Dilley now works longer hours for no pay as an at-home dad, but he doesn't mind. He says, "I'm really glad I got to stay home to develop that closeness with my kids."

As you can imagine, after their birth, they received some publicity after they were featured on ABC's *Turning Point* with Diane Sawyer. They have also gotten one year free use of a van (great for those trips to the doctor, and yes, all are scheduled at the same time). To help pay the diaper bills, Keith and Becki have written the book *Special Delivery*, published by Random House.

"Adjusting to the Instant Family"

BY **CHRIS MONTANO** *Chris Montano is from Lake Forest, California. He is currently running a home business selling a product called "Lift Lips," at www.liftlips.com, to help off-road vehicles look better and cleaner.*

Becoming an at-home dad happened to me rather suddenly. While in the process of a divorce and looking for new companionship, I scanned the personal ads in a local paper and did a process of elimination with the half-dozen I circled. The one I narrowed it down to mentioned that her "Mr. Right" must like children. Being optimistic, I thought I'd take a shot at meeting this young mom. She turned out to be very attractive and had two intelligent, well-behaved, young boys. Everything seemed to "click" perfectly.

We all got along great (a very important factor for the longevity of an instant family). So, after a year of dating and analyzing the potential changes in our lives, we found a house and moved in together while making our wedding plans. I've been self-employed with a home-based business for about six years now, selling a product that I created for off-road vehicles. That took care of one major hurdle in this new arrangement: daycare expenses. I'm amazed at how much some people are paying for this necessity/luxury in relation to their income, and at the same time fascinated with the thought that my grandparents raised seven children on one income and always made it a point to go on long vacations every year.

I've been told by my new wife that I adapted very quickly, and surprisingly well, to our life. I think that has to do with my goal of refusing to grow up completely, for children seem to be the ones that instinctively enjoy every day from the moment they open their eyes. I'm not quite sure when adults are supposed to lose that zest for life, but I plan on retaining it for as long as possible. Besides, the kids like me being a friend rather than just an adult.

Every day has been a new experience for me, from helping out at the kindergarten parties to making sure that their school clothes match and their shoes are tied. I've learned how to get them up, fed, teeth brushed, dressed, combed, and out the door (lunch and homework included) in half an hour. I had the whole process down to a science until about six months ago, when Trina, our little girl, came into our life. Now time is an extremely valuable commodity. Between getting up at 4 A.M. to go to the gym three times a week, changing diapers, running to a quiet room to answer phone calls, making daily trips to the post office and bank, straightening the house, tending to Trina, making sure that all orders that have to go out are ready by the time our UPS driver comes by, washing dishes, picking up the boys from school, making sure they do their homework and clean their rooms and, of course, doing everything necessary to run a business, I go to bed at 8:00 P.M. sometimes.

I do get a kick out of knowing that I know more of the neighborhood mothers than my wife does, and that I'm the only dad in Trina's "Parent and Me" swimming class. The name of that class was changed this year. Last year it was "Mommy and Me." I guess all of us in this position are making a difference in the way things are viewed. We may be rare to a certain degree, but we are being acknowledged. I just wonder if we will ever have equal rights. This lifestyle might be fatiguing sometimes, but I am reminded that I am a very lucky guy whenever Trina smiles at me as I lean over her crib in the morning, or when the boys get excited after I tell them we're going to get an ice cream, or when my wife seems a little jealous as she's leaving for work. Doing the dishes all the time isn't all too bad either; I like the view from the kitchen window—when I find time to mow the lawn. I'm sure there are a lot of fathers who would love to spend this kind of time with their children in their curiosity-filled, developmental years, but can't for one reason or other. At the same time, I'm sure there are a lot of fathers out there who really don't know what they are missing.

"Deep in the Women's Gene Pool"

BY SCOTT BOKUN *Scott Bokun resides in Lexington, Massachusetts.*

I hate swimming lessons. I admit it. Twenty-five years ago, I was the skinniest guy in the swim class, which was a big reason for my bitterness about being naked except for a bathing suit. Now, not only am I the skinniest guy in class, heck, I'm the only guy. Oh, sure, Steven and Mark are male, but they are not potty-trained and do not have a command of the English language. It's just me with my daughter—and eight mothers with their toddlers, all freezing in the lukewarm water of the pool. Swimming lessons. I hated them as a kid and I hate them as an adult. And now I've passed that gene down to my daughter. Before we even got to the pool, I had a sense I was in too deep. As the attendant at the front desk pointed to where the men's locker room was, she yelled to the swim instructor, "Unlock the men's door—we've got a Mr. Mom with his daughter here!" Without missing a beat, I asked, "What?! You don't have a separate-but-equal Mr. Moms' locker room?"

I can joke about it now, but when I first started this tour of duty two years ago, I was a little uncomfortable with the term *Mr. Mom*. There are a lot of dads at home who hate that moniker, mostly because of its negative connotations from a funny movie Michael Keaton did about ten years ago. Other terms are just as awkward— stay-at-home dad (SAHD), househusband, full-time father, at-home pop, male primary caregiver, weirdo with the kids. With today's rampant political correctness, fathers at home don't know what to call themselves.

To be honest, *Mr. Mom* has grown on me. I don't mind being compared to Michael Keaton. (If only I had royalties from *Batman* ...) It is short and gets the basic idea across. Sure, it may lack respect and have a humorous connotation, but, hey, you've got to laugh at yourself sometimes. No need to get militant with the argument about how no one calls a mom in the corporate workforce a "Mrs. Businessman." It's just a name that gives everyone a starting point in figuring out who you are.

Finding a starting point for these swimming lessons, however, is another matter. I hop into the pool with all the other adults while our children stand on the side, the idea being that we can now coax them into our arms and into the water. My daughter climbs into my arms and avoids the water by climbing up my back. With Abby's legs squeezing me like a boa constrictor, I wheeze something to the effect that the pool is just like a big tub, there's no reason to be afraid. I reassure her that I won't let go of her. I try to convince her that it'll be fun, just like at the playground, a water playground. She starts to cry and wants to get out. Sensing that I'm ruining the swim lesson, I carry Abby over to the side and let her calm down. We sit on the edge of the pool in our own, self-regulated penalty box, my daughter now thoroughly enjoying digging her toes into the spongy flotation devices. All attempts to get her back into the water without a fit are unsuccessful. It must be that darn swimming lesson gene.

When we march back into the men's locker room to change, a group of high school boys is in there showering after phys ed class. Some have towels, some don't. (You can see where this is going, right?) I'm trying to get Abby dressed quickly so I can avoid the ensuing embarrassing question-of-the-day. As I tape up her diaper, my daughter, at the top of her little lungs, blurts out, "Hey! He's got a peanut!" As calm as I can be, I say, "A boy's private part is called a penis. Remember?" In response, Abby sings the "Peanut, Peanut, He's Got a Peanut" song. My face is red, but it's nothing compared to the boy with the peanut.

As my daughter's appointed counsel, I later advised her that we could use the popular "she's only two" defense at the court hearing. I was proud that at least she used a name that was almost the right word, not like a friend of hers who calls it a tinkle carrot. Correct word or not, she knew what it was. I had been playing a similar name game with the swimming pool. Big tubby, water playground, swimming pool: they were all equal. And yes, the same can be said for all the at-home dad labels. Different words, same premise. At their heart lies the basic idea of parenting; dads just need to choose the one that makes them feel comfortable. But whether you prefer Mr. Mom or stay-at-home dad or whatever, it still won't change the fact that I hate swimming lessons.

"The Stay-At-Home Dad Blues"

BY CHARLIE LECKENBY *Charlie Leckenby resides in Denver, Colorado.*

Like many stay-at-home dads, I found myself both elated and paralyzed by the idea of caring for our son eight hours a day, five days a week. My wife and I were in the same position many stay-at-homes face: she made more money than I did, and the cost of daycare per month was as much as I was making in a month. We liked the idea of one of us caring for Oliver during the week. It was extremely comforting. We knew that there were plenty of decent daycare centers out there, but still, putting our tiny little boy in some stranger's hands was too much for us to comprehend. So after my wife's four-month maternity leave, I left my job as a software editor and started my job as a stay-at-home dad. It wasn't a terribly difficult adjustment to make at first; I'd been very involved in every aspect of Oliver's care from the very beginning. I was a little nervous about being alone with him for eight hours straight, but I felt confident we would become fast friends. It was figuring out how to keep us both occupied for those eight hours that would eventually make me more nervous.

About half a year into my stay, I started to get antsy. I was beginning to feel cooped up in the house and our routine. I decided I'd better start trying harder to get us out and around other parents and children. I realized I was suffering from separation anxiety—separation from other adults. So we started going to our local children's museum, as well as playgrounds, several times a week. I thought that Oliver would get exposed to other kids, and I could strike up friendships, or at least partnerships, with other parents. I was aware that there weren't many stay-at-home dads out there, but I assumed I'd meet some, and if not, mothers would be a great resource and source of support. I didn't meet any dads at first, but there were plenty of moms. I was nervous, because I thought the moms would be so much better at parenting than I was. Then I realized I was doing the same things that they do, and I had a healthy, happy little boy. But things didn't work out as I had anticipated. Many of the moms were friendly enough, but I began to feel that many of them were not as comfortable talking to me as they were to other moms. It took me a long time to realize that women still aren't used to seeing a man take care of a small child.

But instead of thinking, "Oh well, we'll all get used to it soon," it began to get me down. I began to feel like a freak. I didn't give up, though. We kept going out wherever I thought there would be other little kids and their parents. We joined the natural history museum, the zoo, the botanical gardens. We went to malls and toy stores. But I was starting to feel desperate. I still didn't have any other parents with whom I could spend a few hours a week and talk about what it's like to be a parent. I started feeling like nobody else understood what I was going through. I began to wonder if I was cut out to be a stay-at-home dad.

To compound my developing self-image problem, I started drinking quite heavily. I normally had a few drinks at night, but now I was drinking earlier, and steadily. I was drowning my sorrow with booze. In the mornings we kept to our routine, but I wasn't really trying to be sociable with anyone around me. Besides, it's hard to strike up friendly conversations when you're hung over. I was looking forward to the afternoons, when I could sit down with a full bottle of something and a book, and think: to hell with everyone else.

In December, I stopped drinking and started going to AA. I realized that I was losing control of myself. I was lying to my wife about my drinking, and I was potentially endangering my son. I was so wrapped up in myself that I was losing sight of everything and everybody around me. I realized that I had not truly come to terms with my position as a stay-at-home dad.

I hadn't yet recognized the magnificent fortune I had to be able to spend such valuable time with my son. I was looking at our time together as a chore, rather than a chance to give my son a good upbringing, one in which we could learn so much from each other. Instead of taking things easy, I was always trying to force my will on everything around me. When I thought Oliver would fall asleep in the car if I drove too far from the house, I would either not go or drive as fast as I could in both directions. I also had to stop obsessing about how I thought I should fit in with other parents. Did I really care if other parents liked me or accepted me? I also decided I had to start doing something for myself every once in a while. I'd stopped doing the things I'd done in the past to give myself moments of serenity, like writing and painting. Things that give us a sense of self-worth outside of caring for our family are extremely important. Without them, we begin to lose our sense of identity.

In a way, I feel like I am starting over with the stay-at-home dad journey. Being sober again opens many of the doors I shut during the self-pitying, downward spiral I was taking. I'm still not 100 percent confident about my role, but I'm beginning to feel that it's the right role for me to be in for now. I still don't have many other parents who I can spend time with, but there are a few. And I don't feel like I have to be accepted, or acceptable. I am writing in my journal again, which is both therapeutic and thought-provoking. I'm working on getting involved with some volunteer programs. I hope that by writing this story of mine, other moms and dads who are going through what I was going through can find some glimmer of hope. There's no reason we have to hit rock bottom before we start climbing up again. The way up is always open; we just have to seek it.

"Faxy Lady"

BY ED GRIFFIN-NOLAN *Ed Griffin-Nolan of Pompey, New York, writes the "Pop Culture" column for* Family Times, *a monthly parenting magazine.*

Have you seen the magazine ad? She sits at her clean-lined, Swedish, see-through desk, phone crooked on the shoulder, fax machine gently receiving, papers neatly ordered before her, fingers tap tap tapping a memo—and her hair is, of course, as perfect as her smile.

Then there's the baby on her lap. Baby? It's an ad for God knows what, the thing they want to sell to us parents at home, and they figure the way to sell it is to show us just how good life in the home office can be. This lady is not in the corporate office, but right in the middle of her own living room. She works hard at her job, raises her kids, and loves every minute of it. She has it all; she can do it all. She probably gets wrapped up in cellophane when her husband comes home, too. And the kids fall asleep at just the right moment.

Is there anyone like this alive? How come that kid doesn't scream when the phone rings? Are those papers glued to the desk so the kid's feet and hands don't scatter them all over creation? Who is she talking to on the phone, and how understanding will he or she be when the kid goes bonkers? Where's the formula stain on her blouse, and why is there no peanut butter on the fax machine? In my house everything lower than armpit level has peanut butter all over it. My sons even ask me to lift them up just to smear some Skippy on a particularly hard-to-reach corner of the kitchen. But Our Lady of the Fax Machine pulls it off like a pro. And you can, too, if you just work a little harder, are just a little smarter, manage your time better, and of course, buy all the right gadgets. The subtext to this ad is this: good parenting is just an extension of good management. Look in the parenting magazines—there are more articles than you can imagine that teach you how to manage your time and manage your kids, as if the prime directive in a home full of kids was the same as in an office full of grown-ups: how to keep them efficient and on-task. The meaning of parenting, if you follow this logic, is learning to keep the kids at bay so that Mom or Dad can tend to the fax machine.

A few years ago, I had just finished producing a video short and got a call from a distributor who wanted to negotiate distribution rights. I remember it well. Robert was in the high chair, contentedly dyeing his hair the color of rice cereal while Daniel sat in front of Sesame Street, mesmerized. I calculated that I had about ten minutes before either of them really needed me, and I moved the phone into the kitchen and put on my relaxed, professional voice. I just made it through that call, interrupted once when Robert started to slip down under the clip-on table of his chair, when the phone rang again. A tiny voice on the other end pleaded with me to turn on my fax machine, saying that they had a message for me from the Philippines, where a research associate was based. Since I have to run up two flights of stairs to my attic, boot my computer, launch my communications software, and turn on my fax modem, I asked her to hang up and send the fax in five minutes. I put the phone in my pocket, checked Robert, and bolted for the stairs.

"Daddy?" I almost ran over Dan. *Sesame Street* was over, and he was at my feet, pulling on my pants leg. "Just a minute, Dan," I said and ran for the stairs. There was a thump on the door. It was the meter man. I let him in. Now I had to wait for him to check the meter so I could lock the door behind him, and even then I didn't answer. The phone rang again. It was an editor from a magazine working on an article on Colombia, where I had recently visited. Flattered and stupid, I took the call. Before it was over, Robert had pooped, Dan spilled his juice on the couch, and I locked the meter man in the basement. Daniel was running back and forth between the scenes of these three calamities trying to alert his thickheaded father to the needs that were apparent to a three-year-old, yet I droned on. Robert was falling asleep in his cereal. As soon as the editor had the good sense to hang up, I heard the pounding in the basement, and then the phone, which I picked up, automatically, to hear the sounds of a fax message coming all the way from the Philippines.

No doubt the wizards of Madison Avenue and Silicon Valley may have just the gadget to help me avoid such a predicament, and at just the right price. I choose not to interpret this multilayered disaster as a technological failure. To me, it was pilot error, and no amount of tinkering and gadgeteering would buy back the time lost by trying to do too many things at once. Ads like this one of the faxy lady perpetuate the myth that you can do it all, and keep a smile on, meet the deadline, and of course, keep that perfect hair, the casual look that took two hours of styling to achieve, while raising a pair of Rhodes scholars and Mother Teresas. This kind of nonsense leads to the great American deceit that would have us believe there are no choices to make. Which is not to say that you can't have a home business or any other kind of job and still enjoy your kids. But doing the two at the same time is a serious error, for which you and the kids will pay. And it perpetuates the myth that if you're "just" raising the kids, you're not doing anything. It says to full-time parents that we should be doing something else. And the kids know it. Those real, live people struggling to do an at-home business know that our most valuable asset is a good babysitter.

So get that kid off your lap before she slobbers all over the keyboard or spits up in your photocopier. Knock it off with ads like this that set an impossible standard for women and men to meet. The picture of the stay-at-home parent managing a small corporation with a toddler scrambling around and an infant on her lap is a lie, shaping us and our self-expectations with the not-so-subtle message that we are not doing enough, we should be doing it all (including, of course, buying all the products advertised by the parenting industry).

"A Day in the Life . . ."

BY PETER BAYLIES *One morning a* Boston Herald *reporter called me and wanted me to send him a schedule reflecting a day in the life of an at-home dad. This was written when my son David was five and John was eight.*

6:45 A.M.	John wakes up, everyone is sleeping, he's waiting for 6:59 A.M.
6:59 A.M.	John runs into our bedroom and gets into the bed on my side and turns on the TV.

7:00 A.M.	I am awakened by the blasting opening words of the *Pokémon* show. "I want to be the very best, but no one ever can . . . Pokémon!!" John cuddles on our bed to watch the show, I try to keep sleeping.
7:10 A.M.	Commercial comes on. John goes downstairs and gets his pet guinea pig. He brings it up, puts it on my head. This wakes me up.
7:15 A.M.	My son excitedly tells me that the *Pokémon* characters Squirtle, Diglett, and Poliwhirl are evolving into something I also have never heard of. I still don't get it, and I watch the TV, trying to figure out this show.
7:20 A.M.	I give up and take a shower.
7:30 A.M.	My wife, Susan, who has already gotten ready to go to her job, kisses me goodbye and leaves for her fourth grade teaching gig. Now it's just John and David home with me.
7:40 A.M.	David wakes up and, dragging his blankie, comes to my bed like a zombie. I give John his clothes and he dresses. David is still in his favorite red pajamas.
7:50 A.M.	(Ten minutes until John has to get out the door for his 8 A.M. ride to school.) John has a bowl of Frosted Wheaties, David wants his Frosted Wheaties mixed with "Magic Stars" cereal. The milk has to be just above the cereal so he can push the stars in the milk.
7:58 A.M.	(Two minutes left before his ride.) I throw a peanut butter and jelly sandwich, water, and a snack in his backpack, and he is just out the door with two minutes to spare for his ride.
8:00 A.M.	Now it is just David home with me, still in his favorite red pajamas.

8:00–10:00 A.M.	I set up a small play table for David, and he cuts out pictures and draws while I clean the kitchen, empty (and fill) the dishwasher, and do laundry (which I do once a week). For a few hours, the house is actually totally clean! By five o'clock the house will look the same way it was before I cleaned it.
10:00–11:15 A.M.	David's "belly hurts." I give him some water. I dress him. Today we decide to go to Toys "R" Us and buy John's birthday present. We park my Buick Century in a crowd of huge SUVs. David goes bonkers, since I rarely let him go into one of these conglomerate toy stores that look more like theme parks than stores. David decides that he wants everything in the store and heads toward a huge, remote control construction crane that retails for $89. I grab a remote control car for John and steer David to a freezer filled with popsicles, and he picks one out. Spending ninety-nine cents for the popsicle, I get off easy. On the ride home, he keeps telling me he wants the construction crane. I explain that it costs too much money. He gives up asking for now, eating his prize. The popsicle trick worked.
11:30 A.M.	We're home, I feed David two burritos (his favorite lunch), dress him, and tell him, "It's time to see your friend Allison" (his preschool teacher).
11:50 A.M.	I drive him to his preschool, where he joins around twelve other four and five year olds.
12:05 P.M.	Home alone for two and a half hours! I work on my *At-Home Dad Newsletter* and the athome dad.com Web site. I check my e-mail from at-home dad subscribers and also watch the stock market to check out any trades to make on my

E*TRADE account. I check my to-do list and do the easiest thing on it: "Pay the bills." Two hours seem to pass by in ten minutes and it's already time to pick up the kids again.

2:30 P.M. Time to pick up the kids. I pick up David at 2:40, in a crowd of twelve moms. I try to get David to stop playing in the playground and get in the car so I can make it to John's school in time. David wants his shoes off in the car. I comply.

2:46 P.M. I drive to John's elementary school and wait in the "kids pick-up line." While we're waiting, David reminds me that he still wants the construction set for his birthday. I pick John up, along with three neighborhood kids, and take a LOUD three-minute ride home, during which I hear elementary school jokes.

Joke #1 from my son John:

Q: Why did the spider log on to his computer?

A: To find his Web site.

Joke # 2 from my fourth-grade neighbor, Jared:

Q: How did Michael Jackson get cow manure on his shoes?

A: He did a moooooooon walk.

I've been out of an office setting for seven years. These jokes are funny to me.

3:00–4:00 P.M. I separate my two boys so John can do his homework, putting David in one room with a coloring book and John in the kitchen to do his homework in quiet. He does his spelling test and math homework.

4:00–5:00 P.M. John has three friends come over, and they watch *Pokémon* and trade cards. I play with David.

5:00–6:00 P.M. My wife Susan comes home, asks, "What's for supper?" I either cook something quickly, we order out, actually have something planned for supper, or she whips up something quick. (She can make a full-course meal in seconds; I'm not sure how this is possible.) The kids help clean up by putting the plates in the dishwasher; nothing breaks.

6:00–8:00 P.M.   We play a game, watch a video, or John finishes up any unfinished homework.

8:00 P.M.   Kids go to bed. My wife puts John to bed; I put David to bed. David and I play the "I spy flashlight game," a game he made up in which, in the dark, we point a flashlight to parts of any kids' book, and he tells me what he sees, and I have to try to find it with the flashlight. He loves it and would probably play it until midnight if I let him. When the game is over David lies back, looks up at the ceiling before he falls asleep, and says, "Daddy, I will make you a deal." (I hold my breath.) "You don't have to get me the construction crane I wanted today; you can get me anything you want from that store for my birthday." I'm relieved; I probably just saved $89. But he's such a damn good kid. I will probably get it for him anyway.

Resources

General Resources for the At-Home Dad

Books

A Father's Love, A Daughter's Power by Richard Axel

This book discusses how men handle raising their daughters while their wives are in the corporate world. It addresses the issues that are unique to fathers who are the primary caregivers of their daughters, and handles common issues such as self-esteem and other challenges that fathers can help their daughters overcome. For more information, see www.fatherslove.com.

Adam@Home series by Brian Basset

Basset's books contain a humorous look at the life of an at-home dad. Basset is the creator of *Adam@Home*, a nationally syndicated comic strip. His books include *Adam, Life in the Fast-Food Lane, Minivanity, Life Begins at 6:40*, and *Café Adam*.

Special Delivery: How We Are Raising America's Only Sextuplets . . . and Loving It by Becki and Keith Dilley

After spending five years trying to have children, they had six! In this book the Dilleys tell their story from birth (it took thirty doctors to deliver the babies) to their life at home. Keith Dilley shares his stories of sleepless nights, endless feedings, and his joy as an at-home dad.

Parenting Partners: How to Encourage Dads to Participate in the Daily Lives of Their Children by Robert Frank, Ph.D.

Frank, an experienced family therapist, discusses how to achieve fair-share parenting and discusses the everyday hurdles of childcare. Frank is a nationally known researcher of at-home dads and has done the largest research ever on the topic, with an exclusive survey in collaboration with the At-Home Dad Network.

The Man Who Would Be Dad by Hogan Hilling

Hilling tells the story of how he became the kind, nurturing, and experienced father he is today. The story began when his and his wife's second child, Wesley, was born with Angelman Syndrome, a rare genetic disorder. Hilling devoted himself to being the best dad he could be to his three sons. In this gentle guide, he shares with humor and grace the lessons learned along the way, and his increasing fatherly wisdom.

Dad & Son by Art Klein

I highly recommend Klein's account of his personal journey as an at-home dad with his son, Isaac. It starts with Klein's five years of battles with a rare myopathic disorder and ends with a recovery based on Klein's newfound sense of fatherhood and manhood.

Raising Multiple Birth Children: A Parents' Survival Guide by William Laut

The inside description of this book says it all: "With the birth of triplets, Bill and Sheila Laut went from DINK (double income, no kids) to SINK (single income, numerous kids) desperate for advice, but finding little. Their book is packed with practical tips for parents raising twins, triplets, quadruplets, and more."

Working Fathers: New Strategies for Balancing Work and Family
by James Levine and Todd L. Pittinsky
A great book for an at-home dad thinking of returning to work. Based on research and consulting experience, this book acts as a guide for how men can balance their work and home lives.

Fatherlove: What We Need, What We Seek, What We Must Create
by Richard Louv
Syndicated columnist Louv writes that men must embrace the five dimensions of "fatherlove," including breadwinning, nurturing, community building, finding our place in time and feeling attuned to past and future generations, and spiritual life.

Diary of a Mad Househusband **by Joseph Oberle**
This is a humorous account of Oberle's two-year stint as an at-home dad, starting when his son Seth was sixteen months old. Oberle says the book will not tell you how to be a good house-husband, but it will make you laugh.

The Passions of Fatherhood **by Samuel Osherson, Ph.D.**
Psychologist Osherson is a great storyteller who shares with readers this intimate portrait of fatherhood, filtered through his own family. It includes interviews with other dads on subjects such as helping your child gain confidence, letting go of your children, doubting yourself as a father, and dealing with anger. He writes that fatherhood is "one of the least understood and most mysterious relationships in our lives. . . . We fathers hardly have words for describing the intimate dilemmas of fatherhood, and even when we do find words, many of us choose to keep our passions private."

*Fatherneed: Why Father Care Is as Essential as Mother Care
for Your Child* by Kyle Pruett, M.D.
In this discussion of how fathering affects both men and their children, Pruett, a Yale child psychiatrist, refers to his own study of men as primary caregivers, as well as to outside sources.

Web Sites and Message Boards

DADS-AT-HOME
http://groups.yahoo.com/group/DADS-AT-HOME
An excellent message board for stay-at-home dads, or any parent, to talk about parenting and life experiences. Todd Landrum is the list moderator and Marty Josephson is the list organizer.

DadsList
www.daddyshome.com
A Yahoo! chat group led by Hal Levy of Manalapan, New Jersey, who runs a community of primary caregiver fathers.

Menstuff
www.menstuff.org
This site lists hundreds of events involved with positive change in male roles and relationships. The directory also lists links related to catalogs, men's health, family organizations, retreat centers, youth services, help for divorced fathers, and more.

Proud Dads
www.prouddads.com
Hogan Hilling founded Proud Dads with the belief that the best resource dads have to become better husbands and fathers for their families is each other. This site feeds off the interaction and discussion that goes on between the dads and the issues the dads want to discuss.

Rebel Dads
www.rebeldad.com
This Web site proclaims that it is "the Stay-At-Home Dad Revolution Online." It is a great, regularly updated site that examines the latest media coverage and stats on at-home dads. For more information e-mail rebeldad@rebeldad.com

Slowlane.com
www.slowlane.com
This is run by Jay Massey, an at-home dad in Pensacola, Florida. It's a searchable online reference, resource, and network for stay-at-home dads and their families. The site provides dads with articles and media clips written by, for, and about primary caregiving fathers. It also hosts multiple Web sites for at-home dads, including independent Stay-at-Home Dad (SAHD) groups, all sharing the mission to help dads connect with each other in their local areas. Contact Massey at jay@slowlane.com.

The Annual At-Home Dads Convention

Dr. Robert Frank, an assistant professor from Oakton Community College, has been organizing these conventions since 1996. Since then, Dr. Frank has held a convention every year at Oakton, in Des Plaines, Illinois, on the weekend before Thanksgiving. This yearly assembly of at-home fathers includes devoted dads speaking of their own experiences, book authors, researchers, and licensed marriage and family therapists. The convention is held in an informal, free-flowing format and provides a relaxed atmosphere in which dads can build friendships. For information on upcoming conventions, contact Dr. Frank at DrBobFrank@aol.com, or go to www.athomedad.com.

National Organizations for Fathers

At-Home Dad Network
www.athomedad.com
The At-Home Dad Network is a loose-knit, grassroots organization for primary-care dads who want to start up or join any playgroup or activity to help connect with at-home dads. Since 1994, we have connected and promoted home-based fathers across the country and around the world with our message board, playgroup network, and newsletter. We have no national board of directors, yearly dues, national meetings, or rules. We understand that each playgroup may choose a different level of organization due to the group's location and the diversity of dads that comprise the group. Curtis Cooper, the founder of DAD-to-DAD, who has helped start and organize playgroups since 1994, has integrated his groups into the network. Many of the dads listed in the playgroup network have been featured in the local and national media and have helped connect and promote at-home fathers. Peter Baylies is the director of the At-Home Dad Network; contact him at athomedad@aol.com.

The Fatherhood Project
www.fatherhoodproject.org
This is a national research and education project examining the future of fatherhood and developing ways to support men's involvement in childrearing. Its books, films, consultation, seminars, and training all present practical strategies to support fathers and mothers in their parenting roles. The Fatherhood Project is the longest-running national initiative on fatherhood; it was founded in 1981 at the Bank Street College of Education in New York City by Dr. James A. Levine, and it relocated in 1989 to the Families and Work Institute in New York City.

Resources for Single Fathers

In Praise of Single Parents: Mothers and Fathers Embracing the Challenge by Shoshana Alexander
Along with Shoshana Alexander's own personal story on raising her child alone, this book provides a wonderful account of single parenthood in the voice of real experts, the parents themselves.

The Single Father: A Dad's Guide to Parenting Without a Partner by Armin Brott
Brott gives single dads the knowledge, skills, and support they need to become—and remain—actively involved fathers. Brott steers divorced, separated, gay, widowed, and never-married men through every aspect of fathering without a partner. The book offers essential information and practical tips from experts.

I also highly recommend three books in his fatherhood series: *The Expectant Father: Facts, Tips, and Advice for Dads-to-Be*; *The New Father: A Dad's Guide to the First Year*; and *The New Father: A Dad's Guide to the Toddler Years*. For further information, go to www.abbeville.com/newfather/series.asp. Also check out Brott's personal Web site at www.mrdad.com for info on his radio show and his latest book, *Father for Life*, which takes a look at the phases of fatherhood from the conception of a child through the grandfather years.

Resources for Running a Home Business

Barbara Brabec
Barbara Brabec has been working with and writing about home-based entrepreneurs and craftspeople since 1971. Self-employed for most of her adult life, she is one of America's best-known home business authors. Barbara's books include *Homemade Money*, now a two-volume edition, and *Creative Cash*. Other books by

her include *Handmade for Profit, The Craft Business Answer Book*, and *Make It Profitable*. You can get full information about her books at www.barbarabrabec.com.

Paul and Sarah Edwards

Paul and Sarah Edwards's books include *Working from Home*, now in its fifth edition. A few others include *The Entrepreneurial Parent, Making Money with Your Computer at Home, Finding Your Perfect Work*, and their latest book, *Why Aren't You Your Own Boss?* For further details, go to www.homeworks.com.

Resources for Running a Family Daycare

The Daycare Provider's Workbook by Cyndi L. Beauchemin

Beauchemin takes you through the entire process of starting up and running your own daycare. The book is filled with sample forms and contracts.

Small Business Notes
www.smallbusinessnotes.com

On the Small Business Notes homepage, just type "daycare" into its search feature and you will get nearly all the information you need to start and run your daycare business, with information on daycare supplies, IRS tax breaks, setting rates, how to set a daily schedule, and a business plan. An invaluable resource.

Resources on Homeschooling

Home Education magazine
http://home-ed-magazine.com

Home Education Magazine has been around since 1983 and is run by a second-generation homeschooling family. On this site you will find free online newsletters, discussion boards, a networking list, and selections from the magazine, including articles, interviews, columnists, resources, reviews, and more. *Home Education Magazine* is one of the oldest, most respected, and most informative magazines on the subject of homeschooling.

Homeschooling Almanac, 2002–2003 by Mary and Michael Leppert

From starting out to resources needed along the road, this book covers it all.

To Homeschool or Not to Homeschool? The Complete Idiot's Guide to Homeschooling by Marsha Ransom

Ransom includes checklists to help you out with your kids before they start homeschooling.

Jon's Homeschool Resource Page
www.midnightbeach.com/hs

An in-depth source of neutral, noncommercial homeschooling information since 1994, it is published by Jon Shemitz, a homeschooling dad from Santa Cruz, California.

National Home Education Research Institute
www.nheri.org

The National Home Education Research Institute produces statistics, research, and technical reports on home education. Its mission is to "educate the public about findings from research studies on home education."

Resources on Saving Money

The Complete Tightwad Gazette by Amy Dacyczyn

Mostly a compilation of a newsletter published from May 1990 to December 1996, *The Complete Tightwad Gazette* also has new articles never published before in book format. Dacyczyn is a self-described "frugal zealot" and proves it with thousands of ideas, some as quirky as turning credit cards into guitar picks or turning blue jeans into potholders. The book also has sensible tips and articles on buying food in bulk, cutting down your electric bill, and recycling items you would normally throw away. The book proposes to "promote thrift as a viable alternative lifestyle" and features 976 pages of budget-saving tips and articles. You will easily find a few ideas that will make your money back on this book in a hurry.

The Complete Cheapskate: How to Get Out of Debt, Stay Out, and Break Free from Money Worries Forever by Mary Hunt

Hunt has had great success with her formula for getting families out of debt. She has been in debt to the tune of $100,000 and gotten out of it without declaring bankruptcy. See also www.cheapskatemonthly.com.

Rich Dad, Poor Dad by Robert Kiyosaki

This book reveals what the rich teach their kids about money that the poor and middle class do not. Learn how to have your money work for you, and why you don't need to earn a high income to be rich. See www.richdad.com for more details.

Resources on Do-It-Yourself Home Repair

Home Improvement 1-2-3 by Home Depot

This book is a handy resource. Also check out Home Depot's Web site, www.homedepot.com, and click on "Know-How," which offers free home improvement tips.

New Complete Do-It-Yourself Manual **by Reader's Digest**
This is the bible of do-it-yourself guides. Perfect for the new do-it-yourselfer on a modest income. Filled with color illustrations, with step-by-step instructions for almost any home repair.

Lowes
www.lowes.com
Another great Web site filled with helpful advice. Click "How To" from the main page. The site offers a superb virtual library, which I found very easy to follow, as well as online videos of common household projects for walls, ceiling fans, plumbing, electrical work, and outdoor projects. It also gives you an estimate on how long the project will last depending on your skill level.

Resources for the At-Home Dad Chef

Better Homes & Gardens New Cook Book
This is the famous red, plaid cookbook that everyone's mom (including mine) used. It has been around since its first edition in 1930. This has always been my go-to book for just about anything I cook.

Dad's Own Cookbook: Everything Your Mother Never Taught You **by Bob Sloan**
Sloan helps you all the way through, from buying the food, reading the labels, selecting cooking knives and pans, preparing menus, and even cleaning up. He even offers kid-friendly recipes such as "Six Sandwiches the Kids Will Eat." This is a great, basic, all-around cookbook.

Index

Paranoid Parenting

Why Ignoring the Experts May Be Best for Your Child

Frank Furedi

Named one of *Publishers Weekly*'s best parenting books in 2002.

"[A] provocative attack on contemporary family life. . . . This is not feel-good stuff. But it is a worthy wake-up call for those of us willing to hear it." —*Washington Post Book World*

Paperback, $14.95 (CAN $22.95) 1-55652-464-1

Ex-Etiquette for Parents

Good Behavior After a Divorce or Separation

Jann Blackstone-Ford, MA, and Sharyl Jupe

Written for both biological parents and stepparents, this helpful guide provides the tools necessary to raising well-adjusted children after a stressful divorce. Innovative in its technique and cowritten by a certified divorce and stepfamily expert and her own stepchildren's mother, this etiquette book provides an authentic guide for ex-spouses to interact on a civil and healthy level.

Paperback, $14.95 (CAN $22.95) 1-55652-551-6

Your Second Pregnancy

What to Expect This Time

Katie Tamony

Every pregnancy is different. This is the only book available that discusses what is different about your second pregnancy and why.

Paperback, $14.95 (CAN $22.95) 1-55652-234-7